Introvert's Guide to Dating

Introvert's Guide to Dating

How to Leverage Your Unique Strengths to Connect and Find Love

COURTNEY GETER, LMFT-S, CST

ROCKRIDGE
PRESS

Interior and Cover Designer: Erik Jacobsen
Art Producer: Janice Ackerman
Editor: Adrian Potts
Production Manager: Holly Haydash

Paperback ISBN: 978-1-64876-559-9
eBook ISBN: 978-1-64876-560-5
R0

Thank you, Jenn and Gordon,
for being my sounding boards, and
everyone else who cheered me on.

Contents

Introduction

In modern culture, there is a prevailing message that dating is purely a numbers game and that the odds are stacked in favor of naturally social, outgoing, and talkative people who can form a connection with a potential love interest in a heartbeat. As an introvert, you may feel like you're at a disadvantage when it comes to finding that special someone—after all, you may prefer to spend nights in, devote your social energies to close friends and family, and listen more than talk, and you may even find the idea of making small talk kind of scary.

Not great for finding love, right? Well, this book is here to assure you that society greatly undervalues the traits of introverts, and it will show you how to leverage your natural tendencies as unique strengths when it comes to dating. If you have found dating difficult in the past, you'll learn how to feel more confident and at ease meeting and connecting with others so that you can form meaningful relationships—and enjoy yourself along the way, too. Not only will you gain insight into the science and psychology of introversion, you'll also discover tips on how to feel comfortable in social situations and on dates while staying true to who you are.

Before we dive in, let me introduce myself. I'm Courtney, a licensed marriage and family therapist with a private practice in Decatur, Georgia. I am also a certified sex therapist through the American Association of Sexuality Educators, Counselors, and Therapists, who believes that everyone has a right to live their life as they choose. When you enter my office, the first sign you see says, "Welcome! Come as you are." This is a personal value of mine, and one that is honored by those who work in my office as well.

For more than a decade, I've had the pleasure of working with all types of clients, including those who identify as traditional monogamists, polyamorous, or otherwise consensual non-monogamists. I also work with LGBTQ clients and cis-identifying clients (whose gender identity matches their sex assigned at birth). Early in my therapy career, I worked with refugees from around the world and, because metro Atlanta is a melting pot, I continue to work with clients from a variety of backgrounds and cultures.

When it comes to dating and relationships, I work with both introverts and extroverts. I've helped many introverts navigate dating in this modern, busy world. Whether they are in an innie-innie relationship or an innie-outie relationship, I've also helped introverts in new relationships leverage their strengths and resolve disconnects with their partners.

On a personal note, I am a friend, partner, lover, daughter, neighbor, and cat mom. I am also an ambivert, which means that I have a balance of introvert and extrovert features. While I can appear outgoing to others and can feel energized from spending time with people, I also prefer deep conversations with rich meaning rather than chitchat, I tend to get lost in books, and I sometimes feel drained after too much human contact. I think having experience with both sides gives me insight into the challenges of being an introvert in what can sometimes feel like an extrovert's world.

How to Use This Book

This book is broken down into three parts. In part 1, we'll explore what introversion is and what it's like to date as an introvert. Although you may already have experience dating as an introvert, don't skip this part! Some of what you read will be familiar, but there will be new things for you to consider and great exercises to help you along the way. Part 1 wraps up with ways for you to fully embrace your true self as an introvert.

Part 2 uses what you've learned about your true self to recognize your strengths. Because many cultures value extroversion (and we live in a black-and-white world), introversion is often seen as a weakness. Part 2 will help you see introversion from a different perspective, understand the challenges it can bring, and learn how to overcome them by leveraging the many strengths introversion offers. You'll also find tips, reflections, and exercises to help you put your strengths in play.

Part 3 shows you how to date as an introvert by troubleshooting some common scenarios. This is the part that will really help you find ways to make dating work for you! Together, we'll explore some common problems that may come up when you're dating, such as how to meet in person without getting exhausted after the first five minutes and how to engage in small talk as a way to build deeper conversations.

Finally, please keep in mind that this book is not a psychological evaluation for treatment or a replacement for therapy. It is meant to provide current information about introversion and tips most people can use to improve their dating experience. It's important to note that many people, introverts and extroverts alike, can also have other mental health concerns or conditions, and the information in this book is not meant to diagnose or overrule any diagnosis or treatment from a current medical provider.

So now, let's get started helping you create and form meaningful relationships!

Part One

Looking for Love

Knowing yourself is the first step to finding love. I often find that my clients are trying to bring others into their lives, but they don't know who they themselves are or what they really want. In this first part, we'll review the history of introversion, including current research, and look at some common traits that many introverts share. Next, we'll explore challenges a lot of introverts face, with ways for you to reflect on your own experiences. We'll conclude by taking a deeper look at ways you can embrace your authentic introverted self.

Chapter 1

Understanding Your Introversion

What exactly is introversion? This chapter will provide answers to that question and show you why there's more than one answer. We'll start with a brief overview of the research that has defined introversion and look at the differences between introversion and extroversion. We will also debunk some common misconceptions about introversion and explore how psychology, biology, and culture impact the introvert's experience of the world. This chapter is less about dating and more about understanding the foundations of who you are, which will help when we get to dating in part 2.

Defining Introversion

While descriptions of introversion can be traced back to ancient times (as early as 300 BCE, when Greek philosophers and physicians wrote about it), the word itself was first coined by psychologist Carl Jung a century ago. Introverts, he believed, are drawn inward to a world of thoughts and feelings, while extroverts are focused on the external life of people and activities.

Since then, the meaning of the word has evolved, and while there is no one set definition of what it means, Jung's basic idea is shared by many experts today. (We'll look more at Jung's work and subsequent research on page 6.) There is also a general consensus that, first and foremost, introversion is about energy and whether one feels more energetic with less social engagement or more social engagement. Think about energy as emotional fuel: Like gasoline runs a car, emotional energy runs your body. Some people lose fuel when they're in large or lengthy social gatherings, while others fill up their tank in those situations.

Introversion and extroversion exist on a spectrum. Very few people are 100-percent introverted and very few people are purely extroverted. Many people are ambiverts, meaning they encompass a mixture of introversion and extroversion traits. Furthermore, no two introverts are exactly alike, just as no two zebras have the same stripes.

With all that said, generally speaking, introverts tend to be:

→ Private and reserved

→ Thoughtful and self-reflective

→ People who think before acting impulsively

→ More inclined to appreciate time alone

→ Imaginative and creative

→ Self-aware

→ Empathetic

→ Good listeners

Common activities many introverts enjoy include:

→ Getting lost in a book

- One-on-one or personal time with family or friends

- Volunteering

- Partnered physical activities such as hiking

- Learning a new skill

- Watching documentaries

- Binge-watching shows or movies

- Gaming, especially strategy or puzzle games

Personality is also affected by external influences. For instance, prescribed medications or recreational substances can affect chemical reactions in the body and create specific behaviors. If a person stopped taking the medication or substance, their behavior could change again. Therapy or behavior modification can change a person's behavior. Environmental experiences can also create specific behaviors that may appear introverted. For example, a child who was taught to be "seen and not heard" may retreat to their inner world or start doing a lot of solo activities. This is a learned behavior, though it could influence them throughout their life.

The Psychology of Introversion

There are many modern theories about introversion and extroversion, including those advanced by Carl Jung and Hans Eysenck, as well as more recent researchers such as Jonathan Cheek and Jennifer Grimes. I won't go deeply into every theory in this book, but I will provide a basic summary and key concepts of the most well-known personality theories about introversion.

Carl Jung

As mentioned earlier, Jung popularized the concept of introversion with his studies of human personality and behavior. Jung theorized that a person was born one of two ways:

→ They direct energy inward, exhibiting certain behaviors such as being reserved and shy.

→ They direct energy outward, exhibiting certain behaviors such as being boisterous, jovial, friendly, and quarrelsome.

One implication of Jung's work is that it was an either/or situation, with a person being either a pure extrovert or a pure introvert. But Jung also said that personality develops throughout a person's life.

Hans Eysenck

Several decades later, in the late 1940s, German psychologist Hans Eysenck developed a theory that explored how one responds to the world. Eysenck said we are born with a nervous system that's predisposed to respond to external stimuli in a certain way. He said extroverts have an aroused nervous system and seek stimulation to restore them to optimum levels, while introverts are already overaroused and avoid sensation and stimulation. From his research, Eysenck developed a personality test that's now called the Eysenck Personality Inventory (EPI).

Katharine Briggs and Isabel Briggs Myers

You might have heard of the Myers-Briggs Type Indicator (MBTI), which is an assessment of your personality type. The MBTI was created by mother-and-daughter team Katharine Briggs and Isabel Briggs Myers, who wanted to create a tool that would help anyone understand their personality type and enable them to tap into their strengths.

The MBTI is based on Jung's research and breaks personalities down into "types" based on different traits, two of which are introversion and extroversion. Within this framework, introverts are understood as people who draw their energy from dealing with ideas and reactions that are inside their head, prefer doing things alone or with a small number of people they are comfortable with, and who like to have a clear idea of what they are going to do when they decide to act. While it's noted that introverts may sometimes come across as reflective or reserved, introversion does not necessarily equate with shyness or reclusiveness and people can exhibit both introverted and extroverted traits.

Although the MBTI is widely used by employers and some mental health professionals, there are some limitations to its use as a diagnostic tool, with notable research showing that your MBTI score can change over time. That said, it can be a useful tool to prompt self-reflection and help you gain a better understanding of yourself and how your personality compares to other types.

Jonathan Cheek

More recently, personality researcher Jonathan Cheek expanded on the work of Jung and others to focus solely on introversion, rather than grouping it into a category with extroversion. Most people are not introverted in all situations, Cheek said. He, along with graduate student Jennifer Grimes and researchers Courtney Brown and Julie Norem, broke out four specific aspects of introversion. These are Social, Thinking, Anxious, and Restrained (known by the acronym STAR). When referring to an introvert, they said, you need to look further and see what kind of introvert they are, such as a Social introvert or an Anxious introvert.

If you'd like to find out how you score in these systems, check out the Resources section (see page 167) for links to all three of these personality inventories. Knowing a little more about where you fall on the spectrum will help you get the most out of later sections of this book.

The Introvert Brain

Introverts can experience an "introvert hangover," fatigue caused by exerting too much emotional energy. This is not the result of some sort of weakness. Think about when you put your body through intense exercise, like a really long run. If you keep pushing it, at some point you will begin to have physical symptoms such as nausea, fatigue, sore muscles, or even headaches. This can also happen when you exert too much emotional energy, such as spending too much time in a social situation. It's your body's nervous system reacting to being in a prolonged state of stress.

Although introversion is an energy state, some recent studies have shown that brains of predominantly introverted people and predominantly extroverted people do function differently, especially when it comes to the neurotransmitter dopamine.

Dopamine is responsible for regulating how we feel pleasure and helps with focus and motivation. Introversion expert Susan Cain says the extrovert brain seeks more pleasure and rewards, while the introvert brain does not need that buzz or high that can come with pleasure. They also process pleasure and rewards differently. The extrovert brain experiences dopamine as a quick hit, while the introvert brain slowly releases dopamine over the course of the day. For more information about dopamine and how it affects the introvert or extrovert brain, I encourage you to check out the Resources section (see page 167).

The Culture of Extroversion

Unfortunately, there has been a tendency to view introversion as simply a deficit of more prized personality traits. Cheek sums it up nicely: "Introversion is usually defined by what it is not: extroversion." What the world is saying to us is that if you're not outspoken and assertive, then you're shy and quiet. With this framing, it's understandable why an introvert might feel low self-esteem or low self-worth about their natural personality traits.

Think about a time at your job or in school when you didn't immediately speak up. How did your boss or teacher respond? You may have often heard remarks such as "doesn't participate in class" or "does not engage or work well with others." To succeed, you had to change yourself to fit in with that environment.

How did extroversion become the golden child and introversion the ugly duckling? Extroversion is idealized in many cultures, because those traits are often seen as preferred. Extroversion is associated with taking initiative, being assertive, strong, well-spoken, responsive, friendly, bold, and fun-loving. Conversely, introversion is associated with being uncommunicative, quiet, reserved, soft-spoken, a follower, cold, and even weak. Honestly, none of those traits are inherently good or bad. Yet we often live in social environments that assign such judgments. Therefore, if you're not "good" (that is, extroverted) then you're "bad" (that is, introverted). And no one wants to be thought of as bad!

Ever since personalities have been studied and labeled, those who have what we now call introverted traits have had to work harder and force themselves to fit in. As you now know, energy is what defines an introvert, and all that work takes a lot of energy. It's understandable why an introvert might prefer watching Netflix in pajamas after spending eight or more hours trying to fit in at work. Who wants to meet a date for happy hour where you'd have to use even *more* energy to connect *and* probably in a loud, bright, overstimulating environment as well?

This brings to mind a client of mine named Fiona, who often referred to herself as an extrovert. She told me she took many personality quizzes that placed her in that category. However, as I was getting to know more about Fiona, she seemed to report many introverted traits. For example, she enjoyed time with friends or at parties, but afterward she needed a day to recharge. She enjoyed networking events, but felt drained thinking about spending more time around others after work. She discussed her love of reading and getting lost in what she called "fantasy worlds" and enjoyed taking solo day trips to check out a new town or an interesting place.

She was really good at engaging with strangers and getting others to feel as if they'd known each other longer than they actually had. Fiona also preferred deep conversation over chitchat. Once she told me, "I can do chitchat and I've learned to be pretty good at it, but I'm also okay sitting in silence next to a stranger until something of value is said." She often spoke of how hard it was for her to get going in the morning and wondered whether she was depressed because she needed to just lie in bed for a while before jumping into her day. She also reported feeling frustrated with the dating world, mainly because of the stream of small talk needed to get to a fruitful conversation.

I mentioned the concept of introversion with Fiona, and she took the STAR quiz (see the Resources on page 167). She discovered that she was a Social/Thinking/Restrained introvert, which changed how she viewed herself and her personality traits. Because the world believes that all social butterflies are extroverts, Fiona had just believed she was an extrovert because she did love being with people. She never took into account how much energy she used in those situations and her need to refuel herself the next day. Scoring high on the Thinking introversion section enabled Fiona to realize the source of her fantasy worlds as a child and adult and her strong desire for meaningful conversation. We also identified her need to lie in bed in the morning as part of her personality rather than a sign of depression.

Fiona is just one example of how introverts are forced to fit into this extroverted world. Now let's look at other myths about introverts and see how they square with reality.

Myth 1: Introverts Are Narcissists

Have you ever been told, "You're a total narcissist. You're always thinking about yourself!" Yes, introverts tend to be reflective and introspective, though that is the complete opposite of narcissism. The American Psychiatric Association defines narcissistic personality disorder (NPD) as "a pattern of need for admiration and lack of empathy for others. A person with narcissistic personality disorder may have a grandiose sense of self-importance, a sense of entitlement, take advantage of others, or lack empathy."

After all we've covered, does this sound anything like an introvert? Quite frankly, it sounds more like some extroverts I know. Now, I'm not saying introverts can't have NPD; what I am saying is that narcissism is not the definition of introversion. Remember, introverts are naturally inclined to listen before speaking, which can allow them to be more empathetic to the thoughts and feelings of others. Moreover, they are often quite happy to fade into the background rather than be the center of attention, the exact opposite of a narcissist who seeks out praise and admiration.

Myth 2: Introverts Are Lone Wolves

Many people think introverts like to spend time alone . . . a lot of time alone. This is not completely true. Yes, introverts may need more time to recharge after spending time with others or in a situation that requires a lot of emotional energy, but many do love spending time with others. However, introverts may prefer a shorter time frame for their activities with others, fewer people at a time, or less frequent social gatherings.

Myth 3: Introverts Are Geeks

When some people think of an introvert, the stereotype of a clumsy, academic geek with large, black-rimmed glasses and unfashionable outfits comes to mind. Even the Oxford English Dictionary defines "geek" as "an unfashionable or socially inept person," which certainly isn't flattering. The term is also associated with a person who is obsessed with computers and has no interests outside of technology or academia.

Introverts have their own interests and hobbies, and they spend time doing them solo or with others. When I think of my introverted friends and partners, many of them have fascinating hobbies. I have a friend who takes welding classes and another who creates Dungeons & Dragons campaigns!

A more modern synonym for "geek" is "nerd." However, when you turn "nerd" into a verb, as in "nerd out," the meaning completely changes. Again, the Oxford English Dictionary defines the verb as "be or become extremely excited or enthusiastic about a subject," which is a much more flattering and less negative description. Many people, introverts and extroverts alike, can be excited by and spend a lot of time on a particular hobby or activity.

Although there are some introverts who may fall into the geek stereotype in terms of appearance, fashion preferences, or computer-related hobbies, there are also many introverts who might fall into other stereotypes, such as "the jock," "the princess," or "the socialite."

Myth 4: Introverts Don't Like Conversation

It's not that introverts dislike conversation; some may just prefer a different type of conversation and interaction. When it comes to conversation, many introverts prefer meaningful conversations over small talk and chitchat. Conversation takes up emotional (and sometimes physical) energy. As we've already discussed, introverts lose energy during human interactions. Since that's the case, why would you waste energy chitchatting when you could put that energy into building something of value? Personally, I often find myself skipping the cordial introductions when I'm with my close friends, jumping right in as if "hello" and "how are you doing" have already been said.

Many introverts also appreciate silence more than extroverts, are very comfortable sitting in silence, or may even get lost in their own thoughts or imagination. Think about it: When you sit in silence, it does not mean you are uncomfortable, ignoring, or dismissive. Quite the contrary! You may be completely comfortable and content with the lack of communication. Again, why drive the car and waste fuel when you can just roll the windows down, turn off the ignition, enjoy the breeze, and save your fuel?

Myth 5: Introverts Can't Take the Lead

Introverts can very much take control of a situation. In fact, introverts can make really great leaders because they tend to reflect on situations and think before they act. In our society, someone bold, loud, and boisterous is often seen as a leader because they make themselves seen and heard, but they may also act rashly or silence the good ideas of others.

For the past several years, I've had monthly brunch dates with my very introverted friend Gordon. My role was to check us in on the reservation app so we'd have a table when we arrived. One day, Gordon arrived before me. I greeted him and, in my "I must take control" mindset, went to inform the host that we had arrived. Before I could, though, Gordon told me he had already done so. I was pleasantly surprised he'd beat me to it; it felt great for someone else to take that responsibility.

Myth 6: Introverts Are Shy and Socially Anxious

Because many introverts, and especially Social introverts, enjoy time alone, people assume they are shy. But shyness is a fear-based response that can lead to anxiety, and it can be experienced by introverts and extroverts alike. Often, shyness develops due to experiences or learned messages (such as, "Don't talk to strangers or you'll get kidnapped") that a parent might say to a child. Some clients have become shy after a negative experience in public, and they try to avoid situations that can lead to the same outcome.

My client Ben was a self-described introvert who started therapy due to panic attacks he experienced while at social clubs. He would have classic anxiety and fear symptoms, such as sweaty hands, pounding heart, and a need to avoid places that required him to engage with

REFLECT ON IT

In What Ways Have People Misread Me in the Past?

We live in a society that forms judgments about others. It's a natural part of human behavior. To an extent, it's a survival mechanism from our ancestors to ensure we did not get harmed by others; we needed to quickly figure out who was safe and trustworthy. We still need this innate ability to survive, although not to the extent that our early ancestors did.

In this modern world, people are often judged by how they fit the expectations of others. As you have read, extroversion is often considered the standard for personality and behavior. After reading this chapter, reflect on the following questions:

→ How do I define introversion? What qualities of introversion do I see in myself?

→ How has the expectation of extroversion affected my life, including work, family, friends, and relationships? How would I think about my life and relationships differently if I honored my introverted self?

→ When I ask others to describe my traits and qualities, what do they say? Do their descriptions sound negative or positive? If they're negative, how could I reframe them in a positive way?

others. This panic caused Ben to leave social gatherings early or not go at all. Social anxiety, not introversion, was the source of Ben's panic; it's also what prevented Ben from forming romantic relationships.

On the other hand, my client Jan scored average in most areas of introversion, with the Anxious category being her highest. Although Jan experienced higher anxiety in certain areas of life, she was not shy at all. Jan was a member of the kink community and a leader at a local dungeon. This role required Jan to interact with members every night, including teaching small group classes. However, after a night of work, Jan needed the next day to recharge.

The Highs and Lows of Being an Introvert

As you've probably already noticed, being an introvert isn't bad! There are many endearing and beautiful qualities about introverts that can easily balance out the boisterous and quick-to-react extrovert. On the other hand, being an introvert does have some drawbacks, due to our society's idealized view of extroverts.

This section will explore the highs and lows, or areas of strength and challenges, of being introverted. These are not exhaustive lists, just a few things to think about, and they're not true for everyone; they're based on the majority of introverts. Also note that some of what I have listed as highs could be lows for you, or the lows could be highs.

The Highs

When it comes to the pros of being an introvert, you may benefit from a tendency to be:

→ **A deep thinker:** Deep thinking is beneficial in many ways, including facilitating the ability to solve problems and to have enthralling conversations.

→ **A natural leader:** Because they tend to reflect before acting or making decisions, introverts can make great leaders.

→ **Cautious:** Introverts often take their time before making decisions. This can be very useful when getting to know another person, forming a business relationship, or when weighing the risks and benefits of a decision.

→ **Creative:** Introverts are often highly imaginative, which can lead to creative ideas for things like work projects and dates.

→ **Observant:** Because introverts often sit back and observe the environment or situation, they may notice little details that quick-to-react extroverts miss.

→ **Knowledgeable:** If you're a Thinking introvert, then you probably love to learn. Learning leads to more knowledge, which can generate more conversation and also the ability to teach others. It also makes for a great trivia teammate!

→ **Seeking meaningful connections:** Because introverts prefer quality over quantity when it comes to interactions and relationships, they often take their time getting to know others, whether it's a business associate or a dating partner.

The Lows

When it comes to the lows, you may have struggled with a tendency to be:

→ **Someone who overcompensates to fit in:** Because introverts are expected to fit into the extrovert world, they may inadvertently overcompensate to the norm. For instance, to engage in conversation, an introvert may overtalk and not listen, leading to an unsatisfying experience for all.

→ **Easily overwhelmed:** Too much stimulation can overwhelm the introvert's nervous system. This can lead to distraction or the inability to focus—not the best trait when you're trying to get to know a new person.

→ **Slower at communicating:** Introverts often need time to process information before responding to others.

→ **Cautious:** Just as this is a high, it can also be a low. If an introvert takes too long thinking about a relationship or a decision, they could miss out on an opportunity.

→ **Sometimes overlooked:** Introverts may tend to hang back from the crowd instead of mixing it up in the thick of things. This may work in a classroom when you don't want to be called on to talk in front of others, but it's not ideal for job promotions or trying to get dates.

→ **Not always invited to events:** Because introverts don't need as much time with others, friends or family may inadvertently forget to invite an introvert to a spontaneous get-together.

→ **Seen as flawed:** Because our society can expect introverts to fit into the idealized extrovert world, many introverts are seen as broken and others attempt to fix them instead of embracing who they are.

When it comes to dating, knowing and managing the challenges you face as an introvert enables you to focus on your unique strengths, embrace your authentic self, and enjoy yourself along the way.

Chapter 2

Dating as an Introvert

Now that we have an understanding of introver-sion, let's take a look at how it plays out when it comes to dating. This chapter will explore the challenges and advantages of dating as an introvert. Before we jump into those, though, let's first address the relationship status of "single" or "unattached" and what that means for an introvert.

What Do You Want Out of Dating?

Once upon a time, dating was known as courtship, and it was a precursor to marriage and starting a family and sometimes also a way to form an alliance between families. The concept of dating has changed a lot since then, although it is still usually seen as a way to find a marriage partner. But in today's society, fun, pleasure, and companionship play important roles in dating, whether or not you are looking for a lifelong partner.

As you continue to read this book, think about your own reasons for dating.

→ Do you want dating to lead to a relationship?

→ What do you want to get out of the relationship?

→ Do you want to date to find companionship, such as a travel partner, or otherwise share life experiences but not legally combine your life with someone else?

→ Are you looking for someone with similar personality traits who also appreciates alone time and only needs to see you a couple of times a week or just a few times a month?

→ Do you want a partner with similar values and life goals?

Reflecting on your own needs and desires will help you maintain boundaries and know who to pursue—or not. Luckily, introverts have a natural advantage when it comes to knowing who they are and what they want (which we'll explore more in chapter 4).

The Challenges of Dating as an Introvert

One thing that all my single clients (and friends) have in common is a frustration with dating. "How can this be *so* hard?" I hear them ask. For introverts and extroverts alike, there are many challenges to dating today. TV, movies, ads, and social media promote images of love at first sight and the "perfect" romance. This can leave many feeling daunted by the realities of dating, which are that you need to meet many different people and take time to get to know someone to figure out whether they are a good match for you.

In some ways, the rise of online dating has made it easier to find potential partners, especially for introverts, who can chat with people from the comfort of their own home and get a sense of who somebody is before meeting in person. It has also expanded the dating pool beyond people's own social circles to include people from all walks of life, backgrounds, and communities. However, this brings new complexities to dating as well, especially for introverts. These include the energy drain of speaking with more people, the pressure to be more outgoing to appeal to others, and figuring out how to protect your values and authenticity when dating.

The Energy Suck of Meeting New People

Remember how going to that networking event or mixer drained you after 30 minutes, while others seemed to be going strong two hours later? Remember how you needed a day to rest after a great date, but your date was already planning brunch the next day? As we've seen, the biggest trait that separates introverts from the rest of the world is how they use energy and refuel themselves.

Being around people for extended periods of time, even one person, can be exhausting for the introvert. Think about it: You may be on a date with only one person, but you're still around a lot of strangers if you're at a bar, coffee shop, restaurant, or any public place. You still have to interact with others, such as the barista or the server. Maybe you also had to interact with your date's roommate or family members, if you met them at their home. What was a planned hour-and-a-half lunch date could feel like three hours or more, due to the amount of energy you used for that hour and half.

And the energy suck isn't just about how many people you interact with or how long you are with another person. It's also the amount of energy you use to fit into the extrovert dating world.

The Pressure to Be Outgoing

To fit into the extrovert social world and show your date your eagerness, you may overcompensate by trying to be more forward and chatty than you really are. One client of mine had trouble getting second dates. When we explored what happened on his recent first dates, we realized he was letting his date lead all the conversation and just responding. I suggested he engage more, such as starting conversations or sharing his thoughts about what his date was saying. When he went on his next date, my client tried to lead conversation. But when he told me about it, it sounded like he may have bombarded his date with questions instead of allowing organic conversation to flow from one question to the next or sharing his authentic thoughts about the topic at hand.

Whether my introverted clients are using dating apps or meeting up in real life, I like to remind them that it's okay to ask one question at a time and allow the person to follow up, rather than feeling the need to hit them with several rapid-fire questions at once.

A Tendency to Fall (and Fall Hard)

Introverts tend to value deep connections and privacy. Is it safe to say you don't often reveal yourself to others until a true connection is made? Are you disinclined to go on dates with multiple people due to the energy suck of meeting new people and that desire for deep connection rather than superficial encounters? If these descriptions sound right, I'll bet you are more likely to focus on one dating partner at a time, which can lead to a deep connection.

How is this a challenge, you ask, because it sounds very desirable? Well, if you prefer to form a strong bond with one person at a time, you may find it confusing if a potential partner wants to keep things light in the early stages of dating. A casual approach and superficial romances can seem like a waste of time and precious energy for introverts. So when they find someone they're into, physically and emotionally, they may fall hard and fast.

Often, my introvert clients are blindsided when their dating partners ghost them or choose to pursue another person because the relationship was not going the way they wanted. The introvert may have opened up on dates and shared things that were extremely personal to them but may have seemed like typical information to extroverts. As the introvert, you may feel like you are forming a deep bond, but it's useful to keep in mind that your dating partner may have a different perspective, especially in the early stages of dating.

You might also assume your partner is not dating anybody else. It's best to keep in mind that unless you have a conversation about exclusivity, your dating partner could be seeing other people. Of course, that's not to say it's okay if somebody intentionally leads you on or lies to you about seeing other people. Just keep in mind that expectations may vary from one person to another in the early stages of romance.

Losing Sight of Your Boundaries

Because of the challenges of dating as an introvert, you may try to mold yourself into the person you think a partner wants you to be. Due to your desire to maintain a connection, you may end up disregarding your own needs and boundaries. Maybe you are agreeing to meet up throughout the week when you want to spend more time recharging at home. Perhaps you are saying yes to meeting all their friends a few weeks into the relationship, when you'd still prefer to see them one-on-one. Or maybe you want to protect your privacy but feel pressure to let someone in quickly, even if the relationship is not at that point yet.

Just as you don't need to be the most outgoing person in the world to have quality conversations, you can also stay true to what you're comfortable with without worrying that you will drive other people away. There's no shame in letting someone know you need some space or aren't ready to go to their friend's birthday party. It's okay to take your time letting someone in. Setting boundaries, no matter how big or small, means you are less likely to find yourself in an unhealthy, one-sided relationship.

REFLECT ON IT

When Has My Introversion Affected My Love Life?

To create change, including more satisfying dating, you must first reflect on what is causing your dissatisfaction. This is a great time to reflect on or journal some thoughts.

→ Do any of the dating challenges discussed here apply to me? If so, do they happen with certain people or in certain situations?

→ Do any of the challenges *not* apply to me? If not, why not?

→ Are there any challenges I've had that were not discussed? What are they and when do they occur? What could I do differently to lessen these challenges?

What Might Your Specific Challenges Be?

Now that we've covered some general challenges that many introverts may face while dating, what about specific challenges based on gender or sexual identity?

IF YOU IDENTIFY AS FEMALE

As an introvert, you may feel like some people don't take you seriously, that others mansplain to you, or that you feel the need to take on a stereotypical female role. Historically, women were expected to be quiet, not get angry or upset, and not state their opinions too strongly. Unfortunately, many traits of the introvert *appear* similar to those of the stereotypical female.

When you do speak up or show the kind of extroverted behaviors that are expected of people, others may seem quite surprised and not know how to respond. Unfortunately, many may try to ignore what you had to say and move on without acknowledging it. At this point, you either slink back into the stereotypical female role or have to fight harder to be seen and heard with respect.

Whether you do it quietly or with a hint of loudness, keep doing you. You'll find people who appreciate your qualities, no matter how loud or quiet you may be.

IF YOU IDENTIFY AS MALE

As an introvert, you may be seen as too sensitive or "not manly enough" and may not be taken seriously. How many times have you been considerate of a date and they jokingly said, "What's wrong with you? Men aren't normally this nice"?

Society has certain expectations of how men should be and act. This typically includes being assertive or aggressive, taking control, being emotionless, and being a provider. When a man shows qualities outside these limiting expectations—for example: having empathy, respect, hobbies (other than sports), and wanting to share the spotlight—others begin to question their motives.

If someone questions your qualities as if there is something wrong with you, realize this is their own discomfort projected onto you. Don't let others tell you how you need to act to "be a man." Men can also be gender stereotype trailblazers, and this world needs more men who are emotionally intelligent.

IF YOU IDENTIFY AS LGBTQIA+

Being a member of the LGBTQIA+ community, there may be times when you feel like an outsider in the world, more so if you are introverted. When it comes to dating, there are added challenges. For instance, many people who identify as bisexual report challenges fitting in with the straight, gay, and LGBTQIA+ communities.

Or perhaps you identify as gay, trans, or nonbinary and don't feel like you are outgoing enough or don't look or act the "right" way at social gatherings, where you were hoping to spark a connection with someone.

Another everyday struggle for LGBTQIA+ folx is others not understanding your identity, no matter how many times you try to explain it. Add on the fact that you possess personality traits that fall outside typical social expectations and others *really* don't get it. Or are they just not hearing you because you don't fit into a familiar box?

As a partner, friend, or family member, your job is to share parts of yourself with others, not explain yourself. The people who truly care understand that it's their responsibility to learn more and will do the work to understand you and your experience.

Difficulty Letting Go

Another challenge for introverts can be letting go of relationships that are not progressing or have ended. Again, an introvert tends to only reveal vulnerable parts of themselves to those they feel a deep connection with. This can foster a strong sense of attachment to whoever they are seeing, even in the earlier stages of dating. Although this is an admirable quality, it can lead to intense disappointment when things don't work out and difficulty letting go and moving on to find somebody new.

Remember, it takes a lot of energy for you to form deep connections, and when things don't turn out the way you hoped, it can feel as if you've failed or wasted your time. This isn't so! Yes, forming relationships can take a lot of energy, but the outcomes can be wonderful.

Think about deep friendships you've formed and what those relationships and people bring to your life. Remember, you haven't formed deep friendships with *everyone* you've ever met. It's the same with romantic relationships. You aren't going to form a deep connection with everyone, and everyone you date may not feel a deep connection with you. Remind yourself that this is all right, and honor your needs when connecting with new people.

The Advantages of Dating as an Introvert

Just as there are unique challenges to dating as an introvert, there are unique advantages as well. Here are some of the secret strengths introverts possess when it comes to romance.

You're Inherently Selective

In the previous section, we explored how an introvert may not want to date or even meet several people at a time. Although there are disadvantages to that, there are also advantages. Remember, introverts tend to take their time to make decisions and not rush into things. This quality is very beneficial for dating.

As a relationship therapist, people often tell me that they rushed into a relationship before taking time to really talk about their life goals and what they need from a relationship. They get caught up in the feeling of love, and because they are getting along with the other person, they don't always see that they are mismatched. They end up getting into serious relationships—living together, marriage, children, or business partnerships—and slowly learn that they might not be compatible after all.

You, my introverted friend, tend to be much more selective, thanks to your ability to slow down and think things through. You may realize you truly like this person and you both mesh really well, but you may also realize when you need to get to know a person better before deciding they're your life partner. Your need for space also helps keep things slow. Although you might want to see this person often, you honor your need to recharge alone, which creates some distance. And distance allows for clear thinking and thoughtful decision-making.

You Don't Have Time for Small Talk

Although small talk *can* be helpful in relationships, it can also distract from getting to know someone really well. The introvert doesn't waste time on small talk before getting to the point and starting up a real conversation. It's very similar to the extroverted trait of being direct, though, oddly, in introverts it's seen as socially awkward by some (which, personally, doesn't make sense to me, but I may be biased). This trait also helps introverts make better decisions about a dating partner and figure out if they're a good match, because meaningful conversation helps people get to know each other on a deeper level.

Remember, getting to the point is not undesirable, though I do suggest becoming mindful of how it may come across to another person. Try this: Ask a friend you're close with to role-play with you. Have them act out for you the way you begin conversations with them or others. Pay attention and you'll have an idea of what others may experience when talking with you. This activity can indicate if you need to adjust how you communicate. Or you can just do you.

You Can Plan Creative and Fun Times

Many introverts, especially those who identify as Thinking introverts (see page 7), are great at planning fun activities and have very creative ideas. Researchers Cheek and Grimes discovered that Thinking introverts often get lost in the fantasy worlds of books and have a rich, complex inner life.

This creativity can be an advantage when you're dating, especially if you are living in an area where there isn't a lot to do. It's also beneficial for introverts who prefer to do their socializing at home. Being creative means you can make a simple little dinner party or a backyard barbecue fun and interesting.

Many introverts are also great planners. Although the Restrained introvert isn't up and running first thing in the morning, they are very good at stepping back and thinking things through. If you're a Restrained introvert, then I bet you're known in your inner circle as the planner. If you have the pleasure of dating a Restrained introvert, they will excel at the task of planning things or finding things to do.

You Don't Jump to Conclusions After Disagreements

As I've said before, one difference between the introvert and extrovert is the introvert's tendency to think before reacting or making a decision. In my work with many introverts, I've noticed they also apply this to problems within their relationships. This doesn't mean introverts don't get concerned about conflict or that they are pushovers. Rather, they are often able to hear what their partner is saying and explore ways to resolve the conflict. This also doesn't mean that chronic relationship distress doesn't bother introverts. It does mean they are well-equipped to handle it.

Listening Is Your Superpower

Introverts have a natural tendency to listen. Some of this comes from the introvert's natural quietness, which allows them to sit in silence while paying attention to the speaker. Unlike extroverts, who may dominate a conversation or interject when others are speaking, the introvert creates space for others to speak until they are done. This gives the speaker space and the introvert time to take in what is being said to them. Not only does this help forge more meaningful interactions when dating, it can also help your date feel more at ease.

REFLECT ON IT

What Advantages Has My Introversion Given Me?
Earlier in this chapter, you explored how introversion might be an obstacle in your love life and reflected on ways to create change. Now it's time to consider how introversion has *benefited* you in your love life or your life in general.

→ Which of the advantages listed in this chapter made me say, "Yes! That's me!" When has that happened in my love life? (List as many as come to mind.)

→ Were there any advantages that I initially saw as a disadvantage? How can I see this as an advantage now?

→ Are there any advantages I've had that were not discussed? What are they and how have they benefited me in my love life?

Chapter 3

Embracing Your Authentic Self

This chapter is all about you! Did you just get uncomfortable reading that? Don't worry, you won't be the center of attention; it's about learning ways to be your true self when you're dating. First, we're going to look at barriers that might prevent you from enjoying dating or forming lasting relationships and how you can take control and create your own change. Then, we're going to dive a little deeper into understanding your unique value system.

Don't Stand in Your Own Way

Dating is not always easy and limiting beliefs you may have formed as an introvert don't make it any easier. A limiting belief is a false or negative belief you have about yourself. This kind of belief can hold you back in love and in life.

Some limiting beliefs are formed during early childhood experiences. For instance, "Don't talk to strangers" is a way to help children understand boundaries and safety. What happens if that statement becomes, "If I talk to strangers, bad things will happen to me"? As an adult, this belief may prevent you from talking to people you don't know, which could prevent you from forming new relationships.

Some children form negative limiting beliefs such as, "I'm stupid. I'll never do anything right," or, "I'm not smart enough. No one will like me." These can be learned from messages received from an adult or another child. For instance, if a child is doing something incorrectly, another child may come up and say, "No! That's not how you do it! I can't believe you don't know how to do this already." The recipient may internalize this message and carry it into adulthood.

Limiting beliefs can be formed in adulthood as well, based on experiences and relationships. The good news is that by identifying our limiting beliefs we are able to challenge them and push beyond their limits. Here are some examples of limiting beliefs that could affect dating.

"I like being alone, so I'll always be single." This limiting belief confuses a preference for solitude with relationship status. Everyone needs solitude or self-care time, even when they're in relationships.

"I don't like crowded or bright places, so I'll never have fun on dates." This is a belief that sees dating only from an extrovert perspective.

"I'll get anxious trying to start a conversation and will be ignored or made fun of." Remember, it's not just introverts who get anxious starting conversations; extroverts can feel the same way. What's more, stuttering, blushing, or other signs of nervousness can sometimes show a potential partner that you're interested in them.

"I get tongue-tied talking to strangers and they think I'm weird." This belief assumes that others are judging you for not being a natural conversationalist, when in fact they may appreciate that you take your time to collect your thoughts and respond.

"I like spending time at home on my hobbies. Those won't interest a date." This belief assumes that no one else enjoys the same interests you do. If you conceal your interests, you may be missing a chance to connect with someone who shares the same passions.

"I'm never going to find someone who understands me." This belief prevents you from connecting with others and giving them a chance to learn about you.

"I hate rejection." This belief stops you from beginning to date in order to avoid rejection down the road. However, rejection is part of relationships, because you won't connect with everyone you meet. Plus, everyone you meet is taking the same risk.

REFLECT ON IT

What Are My Limiting Beliefs?

Use a journal or a piece of paper to jot down your own limiting beliefs. Next, ask yourself how each belief has benefited you or not benefited you. Then reflect on past experiences that may have formed these beliefs. Did something happen to you as a child? Did someone model this for you? Did this stem from an experience in adulthood? Finally, challenge those negative thoughts by identifying a positive and opposite thought.

Here's an example to get you started.

Limiting belief: I'll get anxious trying to start a conversation and will be ignored or made fun of.

Has this belief benefited me? No, it prevents me from connecting with others and having a good time.

Source of the belief: When I was a kid, teachers got frustrated when I took too long to answer.

Positive or opposite thought: I am able to start conversations, and I'm allowed to think before speaking. This helps me organize my thoughts.

When It Comes to Dating, We All Have Fears

As we've seen, limiting beliefs can stem from anxiety and fear. Anxiety and fear are not specific to one type of person. At some point in their life, everyone has experienced one or both.

Fear and anxiety are normal responses that are designed to serve a survival function to keep you safe. Think about a time when you were walking in the woods and heard a noise from the underbrush. More than likely, you became more aware of your surroundings, including slowing down or stopping, hearing better, seeing better, and even smelling scents you didn't previously notice. You might have also noticed your body tense up, a quicker heartbeat, and automatic thoughts questioning the location and source of the noise. This response is instinctual. Now, if you're reading this book, I assume the noise you heard turned out to be nothing more than another hiker or a squirrel and you resumed your hike without worry. That was your brain realizing, "All is safe and a bear isn't about to attack me."

What does this have to do with dating? At times, the brain has trouble distinguishing between a possible bear attack and a blind date. Just as you had a fear response on your hike, you may have a similar fear response before meeting a date for the first time. All the brain recognizes is the feeling you are experiencing, not the context.

What you experienced as a bit of anxiety or fear is now turning into panic, which can be debilitating. Some may freeze or feel paralyzed, which is the body's way of trying to keep you safe from harm, though it's not ideal when you're trying to enjoy a craft beer and make small talk.

Keep in mind that fear and anxiety are completely normal. The goal is not to eliminate your fear or anxiety, but to learn how to distinguish a true threat from a non-threat. You also want to learn ways to manage anxiety so it doesn't lead to debilitating panic. First, let's look at some common examples of how fear and anxiety pop up in dating, before reflecting on your own dating fears and how to manage them.

The Fear of Rejection

If you look at a dictionary, you'll see rejection defined as "dismissing or refusing a proposal or spurning a person's affections." Synonyms include "nonacceptance," "abandonment," "exclusion," and "ignoring." Ouch! No wonder we don't like rejection.

When clients tell me they don't like rejection, I challenge them and ask, "What is it you really don't like?" For some, rejection activates a fear of abandonment, which blocks them from recognizing that another person is simply setting a boundary. When you have trouble accepting boundaries, you also have trouble setting them. If this sounds familiar to you, these are much deeper core issues than a self-help book like this can resolve; they'll need to be explored in therapy.

I'll end this section by reminding you that everyone is rejected at many points in their lives, whether it's the promotion you didn't get at work, the student government position you really wanted, or that house where the seller refused your price. Rejection is not a reflection of your value; it's part of a negotiation between you and someone else. It's a choice not to move forward with a plan or arrangement. At times, this rejection or choice is mutual. At other times, it's one-sided. It's never easy, but it's part of life.

Getting Out of Your Comfort Zone

Introverts can get stuck in a comfortable rut, which holds them back from new experiences. But I'll bet the people telling you to get out of your comfort zone were suggesting you do things that sounded like torture, such as going to a "small" party or joining a social group to meet new people. You might have even experienced a little panic at the mention of the idea! These are things extroverts suggest because they think they will help an introvert work through their anxiety and get more comfortable about meeting people. But Summer Turner, a psychologist who specializes in introversion, suggests introverts work on change from within their own comfort zone, rather than trying to feel comfortable in someone else's comfort zone.

Working from inside your comfort zone means knowing what your current comfort zone is and then exploring ways to do one small thing differently, without having to leap out of your circle of safety. For instance, instead of going to that "small" house party, find a new coffee shop that's similar to your regular coffee shop. This will give you a level of comfort while you're trying something new. Checking out a new coffee shop before you go on a date there will allow you to expand your comfort zone without having to meet someone new in a strange place. Throughout this book, you'll find guidance and tips on gaining confidence as an introvert in social situations and on dates.

What If I Get Hurt?

Imagine that instead of reading this book, you are watching me give a TED Talk. It's a dark room, and I'm standing on a stage. You're sitting in the audience, waiting for me to tell you how not to get hurt in relationships. And I say, "Getting hurt is a part of life."

"Wait, what did she just say?" you might be thinking as I slowly repeat the statement with a brief pause between each word: "Getting. Hurt. Is. A. Part. Of. Life."

Many of my clients often report a fear of getting hurt "if I put myself out there." What I tell them is what I just told you. Hurt can come in many different forms, including a physical harm like a broken limb or a minor scratch or emotional pain that may come from disappointment or even rejection. An emotional hurt may affect your level of self-worth and self-confidence. If you want to prevent yourself from experiencing any hurt, then you need to live in isolation where other humans can't reach you. Better yet, you can find ways to manage hurt when it happens.

What do you do when you get physically hurt, such as a minor scratch? You find a first aid kit and tend to your wound. How about when your feelings get hurt? Some of us might get a pint of our favorite ice cream, or journal, or talk to a friend or a therapist. Some people just shut down, which doesn't address the hurt but does invalidate it. The best way to manage and resolve hurt, whether physical or emotional, is to acknowledge it, take care of it, and allow for healing. Not only are you engaging in the best form of self-care, but you are also building resilience, which will boost your self-esteem and self-confidence.

What If It Doesn't Work Out?

This is a common fear, and it tends to prevent many of my clients from taking the first step in dating, which is either creating a dating profile or finding ways to meet new people. However, I've found the true fear is not about a relationship not working out; it's about something much deeper.

Usually, some limiting belief or cognitive distortion (a habitual form of negative and inaccurate thinking) is coming up for them. More often than not, they're reacting to a fearful thought or a negative self-belief to avoid an uncomfortable feeling or emotion or what is seen as an inevitable negative outcome.

Psychologists Scott Waltman and Erin Murphy developed a commonly used technique called Play the Script Till the End to manage these kinds of thoughts. I use it with clients to find out what is really holding them back. I start by asking what comes up when they think about a new relationship not working out. For example:

Client: "Then I'll still be single."
Me: "What happens if you remain single?"
Client: "Then I'll be alone."
Me: "What happens if you are alone?"
Client: "Then I'll be lonely."
Me: "Ah, so the fear of loneliness is preventing you from connecting with others so you won't be lonely."

REFLECT ON IT

How Do My Fears Manifest Themselves in My Dating Life?

As you read earlier, the brain sends signals to your body when it perceives a threat. If you feel threatened all the time, anxiety can become chronic and manifest as other symptoms, such as muscle pain or pain throughout the body, unexplained fatigue, headaches, feeling weak, and gastrointestinal pain or disorders.

Think about times when you were feeling anxious. Write down all the symptoms you remember experiencing and where they manifested in your body. Think about when you are dating. Do the symptoms get worse or better? Do you experience more symptoms at once?

The first step to managing anxiety is to recognize when the anxiety occurs and your specific symptoms. The next step is to learn and practice anxiety management skills every day. These include breathing exercises, meditation, challenging the negative thoughts, and playing the script to the end. Learn more about these from the Resources section (see page 167) at the end of this book, or speak to a therapist about how you can better manage your anxiety.

Your goal isn't to eliminate all fear and anxiety from your life, but rather to understand the proper role of emotions and not let them take over. Emotions are little messages that inform you about something, and you want to become aware of what messages they are communicating, where they stem from, and how to manage them so they don't prevent you from enjoying life—including dating.

For this client, the fear of "things not working out" was about a deeper fear of being lonely, which was preventing them from doing things to prevent loneliness! What I also remind clients is that things aren't always going to work out. We explore times when things worked out for them and times when things didn't work out to compare the outcomes of each. They're surprised to find that outcomes in both cases are usually very similar and there are no extreme consequences, good or bad.

Your Best Self Is Your Most Authentic Self

You probably hear some version of the phrase "Be your authentic self" all the time. But what does it really mean? One way to think of it is the natural version of yourself that your friends and family enjoy being around. Remember, there's never any need to fake an extroverted persona. Sure, it may work once or twice, but eventually your true self is going to emerge. When your natural self emerges, those around you may feel confused or even tricked.

There's no reason to hide the fact that you're an introvert. Nor should you stick to "safe" topics or hide your opinions about things. In fact, people tend to be drawn to people who are comfortable in their own skin. Being authentic allows you to find connection with people who appreciate you for who you are. Not everyone will like you just the way you are, and that's fine.

When you live authentically, you will find that your confidence comes naturally, from within, rather than feeling like you must rely on others for your sense of self. This means you are venturing into dating with a solid base from which to form a healthy and reciprocal relationship where you can be happy with someone without losing your authentic self.

Live by Your Values

A friend once stopped me midway through a "dating sucks" rant to say, "Courtney, you keep telling me what you don't want, but what is it you *do* want?" I'm pretty sure I stopped midsentence, mouth open and silent. She had a valid point: I was ruling out people and traits that I didn't want instead of looking for what I did want. I needed to figure out what I wanted and what values were and were not negotiable.

Here are a few typical core values that people find important in relationships. This is not an exhaustive list, and not all of these values will be important to you. What is important is to figure out which values are important to you.

→ **Family:** Putting family time before anything else. This person may choose a job that allows them to leave in time for family dinners or may limit social time to prioritize family time.

→ **Children:** Similar to the value of family, this person will put their children before others, such as leaving work early for a school play or only dating people who also want children.

→ **Autonomy/individuality:** Having the ability to make choices for yourself without fear of judgment from others. This person may decline Sunday brunch in order to recharge without concern that their friends will be upset.

→ **Tradition:** Doing things as they have always been done and preferring these ways over new ways. This could range from a holiday gift exchange custom to traditional relationship roles.

→ **Faith/religion/spirituality:** Dedicating time to one's faith, such as regularly attending faith-based services or events and prioritizing them over other activities.

→ **Social/community:** Prioritizing time with one's community over other areas of life. This person may tell their boss they can't work late due to a prior social engagement.

→ **Justice:** This is a value of ethics, including fairness, doing what's right, and equity.

→ **Dependability:** This is a value of being trustworthy for others and for yourself.

→ **Work/career:** Prioritizing career or career goals over other areas of life. This person may work late or on weekends to show the boss their dedication and miss other events.

→ **Financial security:** Prioritizing earning money to create long-term security. This person may live frugally, work longer hours, or pick up side jobs to meet their financial goals.

Here is a list of other common values that may (or may not) resonate with you.

Acceptance	Generosity	Personal development
Accountability	Happiness	
Accuracy	Hard work	Quality
Awareness	Health	Reliability
Balance	Humility	Respect
Compassion	Independence	Self-reliance
Courage	Integrity	Solitude
Creditability	Kindness	Stability
Dedication	Knowledge	Structure
Determination	Logic	Success
Discipline	Love	Togetherness
Empathy		Transparency

Identify What's Important

Using a journal, make a list of the values that are important to you. When you're done, think about each value and ask yourself, on a scale of 1 to 5, how important is this value to you? On your scale, 1 is not important at all and 5 is extremely important. Values that you rate as a 5 are more than likely nonnegotiables, while the others are values about which you have some flexibility or may be willing to compromise.

Finally, think about past relationship or dating experiences. Were you living by the values you identified as 5s, or did you make less important values a priority? How would those dating experiences have been different if you prioritized your 5s over your 1s?

Keep in mind that everyone has different values, and there are no right or wrong answers. This exercise is a way to help you identify your own values and begin to prioritize them. Many of my clients who report high anxiety or conflict in relationships are not living by their principles and values. Often, they also judge themselves when others have different values, instead of accepting themselves for who they are and accepting others for who they are.

In relationships, people sometimes try to live by the values of a partner, instead of finding partners with whom their values align. Once they accept their own value system and start looking for partners whose values are more in line with their own, their anxiety around dating and relationships decreases and they report more self (and life) satisfaction.

You must understand yourself and your unique personality and values before you can start using your strengths when you interact with others to form lasting relationships. If you found this section helpful and want to continue exploring your own value system, in addition to the exercise I offered, I highly recommend using the Franklin Covey Mission Statement and Values Builder tool, which can be found at the Franklin Covey website (and is listed in the Resources). Keep in mind that as we grow and change, our values may also change. I encourage people to see values as fluid and not fixed.

Part
Two

Leveraging Your Strengths

Now that you know a bit more about introversion, it's time to look at how you can leverage your natural strengths for success in the dating world. As you know, introversion is often undervalued in our society or seen as less than extroversion. For most of your life, you may have been told that to fit in you must be someone you're not (an extrovert). However, your introversion really can help you in the dating world, and this section of the book will explore six common qualities of introversion that can give you an advantage when dating. We'll also look at how those qualities can work against you—and ways to make sure they don't.

Chapter 4

Knowing Thyself

While being an introvert doesn't automatically make you more self-aware, your natural tendency toward introspection and self-knowledge means you can more easily tap into your authentic self. When you have a good sense of who you are, you also have more clarity about what you want, need, and desire, not just in life but in a romantic partner, too.

On the flip side, when you lack insight into who you are, you may end up dating people with greatly different values, which can make it more difficult to find that romantic spark in the short term and can create tension in the relationship down the road.

Scene One: Tell Me What You Want

Paul opened up to me in therapy about the problems he was facing in his romantic life. He had set up an online dating profile and been on many dates, but his dates seemed more interested in keeping things casual and often sent him mixed messages about whether they were interested. Still, he'd maintain contact with them and continue to date them even though he was feeling very unfulfilled. After one of those dates, he said he was thinking about the date over and over and wondering if the guy will call or text. "At times, it's hard to get my work done because the thoughts just keep coming, but I don't hear from him."

I asked, "Can you tell me more about these men? How would you describe their personalities?"

"Well, they seem quite outgoing and social, and I can't tell if they are looking for a friendly connection or something more serious." Paul began to tell me about a specific guy he had started dating who preferred more casual relationships. He wouldn't maintain contact after they met up for a date, but would "suddenly reappear a few days later as if nothing happened."

Paul did not come across as a casual dater, so I asked him, "What is it that you like about him?"

"He seems fun and interesting," Paul said, but he sounded hesitant.

"Before we chat more, can I ask what you're looking for in a partner?"

Paul opened his mouth to answer and then stopped as if he'd lost his words. He stared at me for a long time, until I finally said, "I wonder if the issue is that you're dating men to see if they meet your needs, instead of finding men who already meet your needs? The first thing we need to do is find out what *Paul* wants and needs in a relationship."

Let's Break It Down

Paul wanted a relationship, but he was unaware of what he actually needed and wanted in a relationship. So he was just connecting with anyone who seemed interesting. If dating and relationships are road trips, Paul knew he wanted a specific destination, but had no plan about how to get there. Instead of researching his route, he was getting in his car and just driving in hopes of finding the destination as he drove. When he saw a place that seemed interesting, he pulled off the road and booked an extended-stay hotel.

In that situation, it was hard for him to know when a person was not a good fit. This was leading to mismatched partners and unfulfilling and frustrating dating. Plus, because he was not confident about his own values, Paul was letting people test his boundaries by ghosting him and then reappearing as they pleased.

Although Paul was the type of person who enjoyed spending time alone and tended to get lost in his thoughts, it seemed that this often led to ruminating about his anxieties rather than taking a deeper look at the issues that were affecting his life. So in our next few sessions, Paul and I started to explore what his values and preferences were. Together, we used the values activities in chapter 3 (see page 40) to identify what was important to him. This helped him find clarity about what he what he was looking for when it came to dating. In his case, it was meaningful conversation, a sense of connection, shared values, and meeting someone who would "stick around the next day."

When he became clearer on this, Paul was able to stop his ruminating thoughts about whether a date was into him (and why he hadn't texted back), and instead ask himself if the person aligned with what he was looking for and focus his energies elsewhere if he did not.

PUT IT IN PLAY

If you have found yourself going on a string of dates but unable to get past something casual and perhaps unable to decipher mixed messages afterward, it's important to check in with yourself and get clear about what you are looking for.

How do you live by your values? Reflect on the values you identified in chapter 3. Perhaps you wrote down "acceptance," "stability," and "community." Now, put these values into sentences that demonstrate how you put the value into action in real life. For "acceptance":

"I am accepting when I_____."

Example: "I am accepting when I don't judge others for their differences."

This part of the exercise helps you recognize when you are not following your own values.

What does it look like when others display these values? To get a clearer picture of this, write an action statement about another person exhibiting the same values. You might write:

"I know others are accepting when they _____."

Example: "I know others are accepting when they don't push me to be someone I'm not."

You might know the definition of acceptance, but you might not know how you or others show this value through words and actions. This part of the exercise takes the values you have identified and creates a concrete vision of how to spot them in somebody else—and how to see when they are absent.

Now, get attuned with the connection between your values and your emotional state. As you did with the first step, fill in the blank using at least one emotion or feeling. For example:

"When I'm not accepting, I feel _____."

Example: "When I'm not accepting, I feel shame and guilt."

"When I am accepting, I feel _____."

Example: "When I am accepting, I feel valued and appreciated."

Now fill in the blanks for when another person does or does not align with your values.

"When others are not accepting, I feel _____."

Example: "When others are not accepting, I feel judged."

"When others are accepting, I feel _____."

Example: "When others are accepting, I feel loved and valued."

This part of the exercise helps you connect actions to feelings, whether it's your own actions or the actions of others.

Remember to check in with yourself. Although introverts are typically very aware of others, sometimes they might forget to check in with themselves. This exercise helps you better understand how you live (or don't live) by your values, but also how to notice if another person is also living by, or at least respecting, your values. It also helps you become aware of how this affects you emotionally, which could help you clarify what a fulfilling dating relationship might feel like for you.

Scene Two: Let Him Go

You met Fiona in chapter 1. Before she started working with me, she would often get involved with men who didn't meet her needs or align with her values. Even in the earliest stages of dating, she tended to put her needs in second place. As an introvert, the many what-ifs of a first date were especially stressful for her: "What if I don't know what to say? What if he thinks I'm too reserved? What if he moves too fast?"

She felt most comfortable meeting up at a coffee shop during the day, where it was easier to have a conversation in a casual setting. However, she would often agree to meet at noisy bars, even though she found it harder to establish a connection and some guys could get a bit sleazy after a few drinks.

After working with Fiona to identify her values and needs and put them into practice, she began to understand herself better and set boundaries when dating. One day, she sat down with a big smile on her face. "You're going to be so proud of me!" she exclaimed. "Our talk on setting my boundaries so I could feel more at ease was so helpful! When I realized my own need to feel comfortable when I'm meeting a stranger, it all made sense. I did what you suggested and created a list of places where I was comfortable meeting someone."

"How has it worked out so far?" I asked.

"Really great! I've met a few guys who were totally cool with the places I suggested and let a few guys go who didn't seem interested in meeting me at my level of comfort."

"And have you thought a lot about those men where it didn't lead to anything?"

"Nope," she responded with more confidence in her voice. "I just let them go and focused on the guys who could at least meet that one need first."

She told me about a man who did meet that need, though the real-life interaction wasn't as fulfilling. "He was a doctor and traveled a lot, but it just seemed like he couldn't talk about anything but his work and how stressful it is. When I tried to chat about my trips to Hawaii, he'd give a short reply and then just go back to talking about his work as if he didn't even hear me."

"So, not your type, huh?" I said with an empathetic smile.

"No, though I did think about giving him your card!" she replied with a laugh. "Seriously," she continued, "I deserve someone who can meet for a coffee *and* seem interested in who I am."

Let's Break It Down

Like many introverts, Fiona enjoyed having some quiet time during the week to be alone with her thoughts. However, this didn't always translate to being in touch with her own feelings. In between our sessions, she started to use her alone time to reflect on her emotions and needs, rather than ruminating about the men she'd been meeting.

She began the same work as Paul, identifying what she needed to feel comfortable dating. Fiona was an introvert who enjoyed socializing, but she much preferred deeper conversations in smaller and quieter locations without a lot of noise. She found it easier to meet new people if she knew the place they were going, and she created a list of New Date Spots that she'd suggest to men interested in meeting her. If a man wasn't interested in meeting this need, Fiona got better at honoring herself and focusing on men who would.

Fiona also got better at recognizing when an in-person date wasn't a good fit. Her date's need to vent about work during personal time clashed with her need for a partner who could balance work with relaxing and recharging. She was also able to move past this experience without it activating her anxiety; she simply recognized that the man wasn't a good fit for her.

PUT IT IN PLAY

For an extrovert, spending a lot of time in their own head can fill them with dread. They may seek distraction in entertainment and socializing. Introverts, on the other hand, are more easily able to find contentment, even tranquility, in introspection. The downside of this (as we've seen with Paul and Fiona) is that *too much* contemplation can lead to unproductive worry and rumination.

The next time you are alone with your thoughts, instead of playing over scenes from past dates or worrying about future dates, try directing your attention to considering what your values are, what you're comfortable with, and what boundaries you can put in place.

The following questions are a good starting point.

→ **Where I am most comfortable meeting people?** If you find first dates stressful, try writing up a list of New Date Spots where you are most at ease meeting people.

→ **What are my deal-breakers on a date?** Is it someone who talks over you? A person who doesn't listen and only talks about themself? Someone who moves too fast? Get to know the red flags that somebody may not be a great fit for you.

→ **When do I cut my losses?** Are you sending clear follow-up messages after a date and not getting any response? Is your date sending mixed messages? Be honest with yourself about what you're okay with and what you're not. If you realize the situation isn't working for you, give yourself permission to let it go.

→ **What am I looking for?** This may seem obvious, but take the time to ask yourself what you are really looking for and stay true to that. If you are trying to make a meaningful connection that leads to a serious relationship but the person you're seeing seems more interested in Netflix and chill, it may be time to look elsewhere.

Another exercise you can use is what I call People-Watching from the Outside In. When you're people-watching in a public place like an airport or a mall, you observe what others are doing and you might even create your own story about them, based on how they wear a certain new fashion or how they interact with other people. In this exercise, instead of watching others, though, you are going to people-watch yourself.

First, think about a recent date you had. Write a story about the date as if you are a bystander watching from another table or the proverbial fly on the wall. Write out everything you can remember, from how each person was sitting to the tone of voice or facial expressions you observe. When it's all written down, read the scene as if you are a people-watching bystander, not a character in your own story.

→ What do you see happening between the two characters?

→ Do you notice either character acting a certain way? More important, what do you see *your* character doing?

→ Would you have done anything differently?

REFLECT ON IT

In this chapter, you've learned that being an introvert who enjoys quiet time with their own thoughts doesn't necessary translate to being clear about your feelings, values, and boundaries. Moving forward, consider how you can use downtime to your advantage by getting clear about what's important to you, both on a personal level and in terms of what you want from a partner. As you do, reflect on the following questions, putting pen to paper if you'd like.

→ What are my core values and how do I need these to be respected?

→ What does it look like when a romantic interest displays these values?

→ How can I become more aware of when somebody isn't meeting my needs?

→ How can I set boundaries in a different way?

→ How might these actions change my experiences, in dating and in long-term relationships?

Chapter 5

Selectiveness Is a Virtue

Introverts tend to take their time before making decisions. They are also typically more observant, carefully assessing a scenario and noticing the smaller details that more impulsive extroverts may miss. When it comes to dating, the ability to slow down and make a careful decision can be a superpower for introverts. As you'll learn in this chapter, the trick is to make sure you are making decisions for the right reasons.

Scene One: Don't Rush

We're not done with Fiona. After getting in touch with her values and setting better boundaries, Fiona began to ease into dating. She was dating guys who were much better suited to her, but still couldn't seem to find that the right chemistry. "Don't get me wrong," she told me one day. "I've met some really awesome guys and am having fun on dates. But I just haven't found that special spark I'm looking for."

"Do you feel pressure to be in a relationship?" I asked Fiona.

"I suppose so," she replied, "I've been single for a year now, and sometimes it feels like I'll never meet the right person. It's funny, my friends used to tell me I needed to cut my losses when I saw red flags with guys, rather than going on more dates with them. But this week they said that maybe now I'm being too picky."

"Perhaps it's better to take your time to find the right match, rather than rushing into a romance with the wrong person," I suggested.

"That's true. I suppose I shouldn't be so hard on myself."

We talked about reframing the idea of "being picky" (a negative trait) into "being selective" in a healthy way to find someone who aligns with your values and needs. When she started thinking back to when she ended up in relationships with men who were totally a mismatch, Fiona felt more relaxed about taking her time to meet the right person.

Let's Break It Down

There's an old saying that fools rush in where angels fear to tread. In other words, rash decisions are rarely the best. Something I learned growing up was to sleep on it before making a big decision, such as a large purchase or something life-changing like a new job or a move. Often, rash decisions are made from the part of our brain that depends on survival. Quick decisions are needed in life-or-death situations, but dating, thankfully, does not fall into that category. We can slow down and think about our choices. The trick is to make decisions for the right reasons.

For Fiona, this meant making judgments based on her values and needs. When people rush into a relationship too fast, it can often be a choice that's based in fear. Perhaps a fear of loneliness or of "running out of time" (especially if your friends are pairing off), or worrying that if you break it off with whoever you are seeing you may not find somebody better.

However, when you focus on your values and needs, you are able to slow down and use your decision-making superpower to clearly assess dating situations. That way, you can consciously choose to go out with a person because they fit into your world. I guarantee the experience will be much more enjoyable than dating out of fear!

PUT IT IN PLAY

Introverts are selective, not picky. Picky implies judgmental; selective implies careful and assertive. Words are a powerful thing.

If one is told from an early age that they are too picky and hard to please, they may form a limiting belief that they aren't good enough to get what they really want, including dating and finding a partner. However, if you encourage a child to be selective, they will slow down and take their time (or use their natural introvert superpower) to make a well-considered decision. They will also feel confident in the decisions they make, such as choosing to date one person at a time or not rushing into a relationship to meet a need or alleviate a fear.

Now I want you to think about the language you use to describe yourself.

→ Is that language limiting in any way? If so, how?

→ Does it paint you in a poor light?

→ Do negative emotions come up when you hear the word "picky" (or a similar term)?

If you said "yes" to any of these questions, reframe the language you use to describe yourself. For instance:

→ Instead of bossy, you are assertive.

→ Instead of anxious, you are cautious.

→ Instead of slow, you are patient.

→ Instead of shy, you are thoughtful.

→ Instead of nerdy, you are intelligent.

→ Instead of rude, you are direct.

You can use any or all of my reframes, or come up with your own. When you're done, say each one out loud. For example, "I'm not shy, I'm thoughtful." When you catch yourself applying negative labels to yourself in everyday life, use these reframes. Do this every day until that new language becomes a part of your core beliefs.

Scene Two: I Know What I Know

Caryn was frustrated by the dating scene. "There is just no one available these days," she told me with a resigned look on her face. As we talked further, I began to realize that Caryn was chatting with a lot of people online, and all those connections fizzled out instead of resulting in a first date. Caryn began to suggest she might "just be single and focus on other goals in life" instead of finding a partner.

When I asked her why she thought her conversations didn't progress into dates, she simply said, "I wasn't interested," or, "They're just not my type."

"And what is your type?" I asked.

"I'll just know when I know," she said.

Another client, Joaquin, reported going out with several women he met and having a really great time. He told me after each date he was excited to see the person again. They'd have some ongoing conversation between dates, but after a few weeks or a month, the woman would typically break it off. He said they often told him "I was coming on too strong or looking for something more serious than they wanted."

"Why do you think women would get that impression?" I asked.

Joaquin told me he could see these matches as potential future partners and began to envision how they might take a vacation or celebrate holidays together. As he talked, I could see that this vision was likely one-sided. Joaquin was behaving as if there was a serious connection, while the women he met were dating more casually and taking things slowly, where two people organically get to know each other.

Let's Break It Down

For some introverts, intuition allows them to have a strong inner sense of self and an idea of what they want without having to consciously think about it or put it into words. Often, introverts just know someone is right for them—or wrong for them—after one conversation.

Caryn had an idea or feeling of what she was looking for, although she couldn't articulate it. Her trust in her intuition led her to dismiss the men she met without even giving them a chance, if they didn't seem to be an ideal partner. In other words, Caryn was judging books by their covers and not at least reading a few pages before deciding to put them down.

On the other hand, Joaquin got caught up in his own vision of who his date was instead of seeing each woman and each situation as they were. Jenn Granneman writes in *The Secret Lives of Introverts* that the introvert's imagination can quickly idealize a person they just met, and then they see this person only through a lens that is turned inward. Which is to say, the tendency to inhabit a rich inner world can lead to romanticizing a love interest without seeing the reality of who they are.

When you meet someone new and fall in love, you activate a part of the brain that isn't rational. When this is combined with the active inner world of a typical introvert, you really can't see things clearly! But when you don't actually see the person you're dating, it can be a big turnoff for them.

Although selectiveness can be a superpower, it can also create some barriers and some heartbreak. Let's look at ways to make sure selectiveness remains an advantage, rather than an obstacle.

→ **Be open to at least an intro date.** I always tell clients who are unsure about a match, "Just go on the date, anyway. If nothing else, you'll enjoy some company and can practice your social skills."

→ **Don't set your sights on one person.** If you're comfortable with it, dating more than one person at a time can help curb the overactive imagination, because you have more than one person to think about and put your energy toward.

→ **Keep things real—as in realistic.** Introverts can sometimes fall head over heels for someone they barely know and create an idealized relationship in their inner world. Write about your date and then take a look at it the next day; this can help you to see things from a different perspective. Does it still look the same as it did yesterday?

→ **Listen to your friends (or therapist)—they're probably right.** When we're blinded by love, we're viewing things through a fantasy lens. However, others in our life may see things from a more realistic perspective. If many of your friends are telling you the same thing, take a step back and give yourself some space from your new love interest. With a little bit of time, your reality lens will come back into focus and you'll see things much more clearly.

→ **Slow things down.** All the suggestions here can help slow things down. Also slow it down by keeping yourself busy with other hobbies, interests, and friend dates.

REFLECT ON IT

Selectiveness can be very handy in decision-making in all areas of life. As an introvert, you can leverage your natural tendency to be more cautious and deliberate to make the best decisions when it comes to dating. However, left unchecked, these tendencies can hinder you if you become too selective or aren't clearly aware of what you are looking for.

Think about how you are selective in your dating life.

→ In what ways has being selective helped me?

→ In what ways has it held me back or created barriers?

→ How would it feel to change the perception of myself as "picky" and embrace the idea of being thoughtfully "selective"?

→ Could I ask a friend or trusted confidant for their unbiased feedback? Based on their feedback, how do I see that being selective has created more benefits in my life?

Chapter 6

The Art of Listening

It's likely you've been told more than once that you're a good listener. This is probably in contrast to the extroverts in your life, who tend to be the sort of people who are energized by being around others and are clamoring to get every thought out of their head. If you're more focused on your internal world, you don't feel the need to "think out loud" when you are around others. This naturally makes you a better listener. As we'll explore in this chapter, this can give you a leg up when it comes to dating and relationships, as long as you use it to your advantage.

Scene One: Sitting in Silence

Being quiet doesn't mean you're not paying attention. I often tell people, "If you don't want me to remember it, then don't say it in front of me." I'm notorious for remembering everything I hear, even if it's not said to me directly. I can't tell you how many times I've surprised others with a detailed recollection of a conversation from years in the past. My quietness and memory archive help me to be a good therapist, and have come in handy with getting to know people in a social context such as dating.

When I'm out with an extrovert, you'll usually find me sitting quietly and attentively showing interest while my date is excitedly sharing something. You'll see me responding only when they are done. I might share a similar experience or reflect back what they said and how I heard it. As an introvert with an active inner world, sitting and listening to my date share stories is natural for me and I enjoy it. Instead of reading a book, it's like the book is being read to me by the character himself.

When I'm out with another introvert, the scene is much different. At times, it takes a moment to get the conversation going while we both figure out who is going to speak first. With my introvert dates, there is often more quiet time and less expressive conversation. We don't need to exaggerate to get our point across or connect with each other. Our proclivity toward calmness and quiet also allows us to sit in more silence, without the need for conversation to fill every moment.

Let's Break It Down

Adam McHugh, author and contributor to Introvert, Dear (an online community for introverts), describes the introvert's natural strength of listening as the ability to be hospitable to another's thoughts and feelings. When you are speaking to a romantic interest online or IRL, you're stepping out of your internal world and welcoming the experience of learning more about someone else and forming a connection.

As an introvert, your natural inclination is typically to absorb information into your own world and put that new information into a memory file to recall at another time. In the flow of conversation, this often means that your introvert brain isn't working overtime to form your next response or interject with your own thoughts, as the extrovert's brain might be. Instead, you're breaking down the information that was just provided in your head while also actively listening to the speaker. Those in conversation with you often find it nice not to be interrupted, as excited extroverts often do. As a natural listener, you may give an unspoken message of, "I am interested in what you have to say, and I'm patient enough to wait until you are finished to share my own thoughts on the topic."

PUT IT IN PLAY

Listening is an art. Although your skill as a natural listener can help create a connection by sending messages that you are interested in the other person, too much listening without enough back-and-forth conversation could send the exact opposite message—that you aren't interested.

Steven R. Covey, author of *The Seven Habits of Highly Effective People*, talks about the ability to listen to understand and the ability to listen to respond. Listening to understand is the ability to absorb information without actively thinking about your own response. This is about understanding the speaker's experience and providing validation for what they are sharing. Listening to respond is the art of absorbing new information while formulating your own thoughts in response to what you have been provided by the speaker.

Introverts tend to be good at listening to understand but not as good at listening to respond. Here are some helpful techniques to help you both understand and respond.

Practice nonverbal body language. When I started making videos for my podcasts, I noticed my body language did not match the excitement or curiosity I knew I had experienced. I started practicing which facial features went with emotions and tried extra hard to show those during filming. For example:

→ A huge smile can indicate excitement or pleasure.

→ Raised eyebrows can show intrigue or surprise.

→ An open mouth can show shock, excitement, or surprise.

Be careful of body language that could give the wrong message, such as:

→ Squirming or moving too much can show nervousness or discomfort.

→ A blank stare can show disinterest or ignoring.

→ Looking away can show disinterest.

Balance listening and speaking. When you're getting to know someone, it's important to balance talking and listening. Silence is great to show how you can be attentive and allow your date to share their thoughts. However, too much silence might send a message that you are not interested. Show your date that you are interested by asking questions about their experiences, sharing a similar story, and remaining focused on them instead of distractions such as a phone or other people around you. If the topic does not seem interesting, try introducing a topic with more significance or a deeper meaning for you.

Come prepared with conversation. Although you may not like small talk or chitchat (we'll explore this more in chapter 7), coming to a date with a handful of conversation topics can help put you at ease when forming a new connection. You might want to write down a list of topics and a few bullet points of interest around each. Perhaps it's a shared interest or hobby you've noticed on their dating profile or talking about your latest travels. Just make sure they are topics you can share your thoughts on, rather than simply a list of questions to ask your date.

Scene Two: What Does Listening Look Like?

Priya, a self-identified extrovert, and Gabriella, a self-identified introvert, came to relationship therapy to address communication issues. Although they had been together for a while, this problem began early on. Like many, they thought it would work itself out, which rarely is the case. They got to a point where they were considering ending their relationship and agreed to see if therapy could help.

"I just don't believe she actually listens to me," Priya adamantly stated while crossing her arms and glancing sideways at Gabriella.

"I listen to her," Gabriella calmly stated without any other emotion and body language.

Priya didn't have to say anything for me to read her facial expression, which said she did not believe this. "Can you give me an example of when you don't believe Gabriella is listening to you?" I asked.

"Sure. Ever since we started dating, I'll tell her things, and she barely seems to look up from what she's doing. No emotion, no facial expression, no words. Nothing!" Priya was getting more exasperated and frustrated as she recalled the many times her introverted partner hadn't responded to her.

"What? Do you want a neon sign to light up after everything you say to me?" Gabriella asked, now showing some emotion around her frustration.

"Hold up," I interjected before things got out of hand. "I'd like to know more about your experiences in conversation, including both of your expectations for speaking and listening."

I met with each separately, to allow them to speak freely without creating more tension. I learned that, in Gabriella's words, her extroverted partner "tends to ramble and talk a lot. Sometimes it seems she's just talking to talk and not speaking to anyone in particular. It's hard to know *if* I should be listening. Honestly, I don't have to say much to hear what another person is saying. I do this with everyone, though she seems to take it personally. The crazy thing is, I always follow through when she asks things of me, and I can repeat back what she says."

When I met with Priya, she spoke about trying to connect with her introverted partner through conversation, such as sharing her day or interesting things she had learned. "This is just how I connect with people, and I don't seem to have this problem with other people in my life."

Let's Break It Down

After talking to Priya and Gabriella together and separately, I started to understand what was happening. This was a classic example of what happens in relationships where one partner is an extrovert and the other is an introvert. Priya and Gabriella didn't have communication issues; they were simply communicating with each other in their own ways.

Priya was trying to interact with Gabriella as an extrovert, and Gabriella was interacting with Priya as an introvert. Although Gabriella wasn't interjecting comments during conversation, it didn't mean she wasn't listening. She was silently engaging, and she did respond or comment when she thought it was needed. As Gabriella pointed out, she would often follow through on Priya's requests, even though she would not say this is what she planned to do. But to Priya, this felt like she was being ignored.

As you may recall from chapter 3, when a person experiences anxiety or stress, they move into the survival mode part of the brain, which may prevent them from seeing small details in their environment, such as things their partner is doing. Priya's high anxiety around the relationship distress caused her to miss seeing when Gabriella did follow through on issues brought up in their conversations. Priya was not seeing how Gabriella was listening to her.

When I brought them back together, I shared with them my insights and observations of how they communicated and their personal expectations around communication. I pointed out that Priya expected others to actively engage in conversation and directly state their intention to follow through, while Gabriella didn't need to use a lot of words or even nonverbal communication to take in information and didn't feel the need to share her plan to get things done. As I talked, they both emphatically nodded in agreement and began to look calmer. They were finally beginning to understand their very different communication styles.

PUT IT IN PLAY

Active listening is a simple technique to help couples with different communication styles, and it doesn't require either person to completely change the way they do things. It involves both mindful listening and eye contact to show that one is listening, as well as clarifying comments or paraphrasing what was heard to ensure the correct message is received.

I encouraged Priya and Gabriella to practice active listening using the following strategies.

→ **Distraction-free time:** There are times when it's okay to have a conversation while multitasking, such as folding the laundry, cooking meals, or driving in the car. There are other times when your partner will want your undivided attention. Encourage them to express that need with statements such as, "I need to talk to you about _____. When do you have a moment that you're not busy?" Then set aside distraction-free time when you can give your partner your undivided attention.

→ **Attention:** Although you might be busy or trying to get something else done, be sure to let the other person know they have your attention. This can be done by:

▸ Maintaining eye contact during the conversation

▸ Setting other tasks aside for a moment

- Verbally letting the other person know you are actively listening

→ **Clarification and paraphrasing:** To ensure you're on the same page with your partner, it's best to repeat back what you heard. This will avoid unintentional conflict if one of you heard something different. For example:

- "What it sounds like you need is _____."

- "I can help out with _____. I'll put that on my to-do list for tomorrow."

REFLECT ON IT

For most introverts, their natural inclination is to listen rather than talk over people. This gives you an advantage when it comes to getting to know somebody, especially in contrast to your extroverted counterparts. However, when you listen without reciprocating in conversation or fail to show your excitement or interest with verbal and nonverbal cues, you may be misunderstood.

Think about how you currently listen to others on dates.

→ Do I tend to listen to absorb or to respond?

→ When does listening to respond work out better for me and when does listening to absorb work out better?

As you go on the next few dates, pay attention to how you listen and the listening skills you're using. Review the suggested techniques to improve your listening and response skills. Ask yourself:

→ Which skills am I currently using and excel at?

→ Which ones could I improve on?

Chapter 7

Don't Fake Small Talk

Conversation is the cornerstone of forging connections when you're dating. As an introvert who likely has an aversion to meaningless small talk, you've probably considered this a challenge. As you'll learn in this chapter, the trick to navigating this trait on a date is not to fall into the trap of faking extroversion, like trying to be outgoing by talking about anything and everything or asking a million questions. Rather, you can leverage your natural inclination for meaningful conversation to attract and connect with people you're interested in.

Scene One: A Man of Few Words

Tyler came to see me after a long-term relationship ended and he began dating again. He hadn't dated in more than a decade and was unsure of how to go about it now that he was single again.

Tyler was a man of few words, as I found out in session after session. He would often get straight to the point when entering my office and provide very short and simple answers to my questions. We discussed ways he could begin to meet women and explored his own needs in a new relationship. One day, he came in looking very confused and frustrated.

"What's on your mind?" I asked, getting to the point, as I had learned that chitchat was not his thing.

"This dating thing is more frustrating than it's worth! I can't seem to get anyone to respond to my messages! I mean, why do people sign up for dating apps if they're not even going to talk?!"

"Tell me more about the interactions. For instance, what type of messages are you sending women?" I asked.

"You know, the general, 'Hey, what's going on?' or, 'What are you up to this weekend?'"

"That sounds like small talk to me," I replied, tilting my head and raising my eyebrows to signal my curiosity. I gave him a moment to think about that before saying, "In the short time we've known each other, I've learned you're not the small talk type and prefer getting to the point and not wasting words. Am I wrong?"

"Yeah, that's pretty accurate. I thought that's how you're supposed to start a conversation with others . . ." He let the words trail off—not a statement and not quite a question.

"Sure. It's *one* way you can start a conversation. Though you can also start one by focusing on a shared interest you both have or asking about a picture they posted. You could also share something about yourself that isn't in your profile."

Tyler seemed less confused and frustrated, though I hadn't totally convinced him that being true to his own communication style could actually help him meet women. I continued, "Instead of trying to fit into what everyone else does, have you considered how you can use your desire for intentional conversation to help you stand out and get more responses?"

Let's Break It Down

Before I share the exercise Tyler and I did, let's first take a look at what happened when he started online dating. Tyler was falling into the trap of trying to fit into the extrovert world, instead of using his ability to engage in meaningful conversation to his advantage. As an introvert, you're well aware of how extroverts expect you to communicate in their style. Like Tyler, you probably learned how to make basic small talk to fit in, but this doesn't help you stand out if others are receiving similar small talk messages. If someone is an introvert like you, then to them you look like another extrovert, when what they probably want is deeper and more genuine opening conversations.

Tyler was not using his strength of making more intentional conversation, and instead was trying to make small talk. The result was that women were not responding to his messages, which does happen with dating apps if one doesn't stand out from the crowd. Although Tyler *could* have meaningful conversations, as he did in our sessions, he was getting stuck in the dating scene because he was being inauthentic, which was causing him frustration with the whole dating process. He also might have been missing connections with those who were looking for a deeper conversation style.

PUT IT IN PLAY

Now let's look at an exercise I used with Tyler that can help you if you've ever found yourself in a similar situation with online dating.

Identify topics for deeper conversation. Find a person who intrigues you, pull up their profile, and identify some unique things about them that you find interesting. For Tyler, this was a woman named Sonya, who had pictures of herself on trips and being active; said she enjoyed gaming, hiking, brunch, and trying out golf; and was interested in meeting for a long-term relationship.

Now, imagine this person on your app is someone you already know. How might you start the conversation, knowing these specific things about them? For instance, do they have an interest that you also know something about? Travel photos from somewhere you've been or want to go? Alternatively, imagine this was your profile. What message would you want this person to send you?

Think up alternatives to small talk. Once you've identified topics of conversation, try drafting a message reaching out to them that bypasses vague chitchat. Tyler saw that Sonya was a hiking enthusiast who enjoyed traveling and the outdoors as much as he did. After talking it out, I helped Tyler put everything into words, and this is the message he created.

> Hey Sonya! Your travel photos are amazing. Where did you go hiking? I just visited a national forest in North Carolina for a weekend getaway myself.

Be sure to share your interests with others. Of course, conversation is a two-way street, so be sure to include enough information about yourself on your dating profile to spark interest from others. It may be your field of work, your hobbies, what you enjoy learning about, some trivia about yourself—anything that can help you seem like a relatable and compelling person to chat with, rather than just another face. You may, after all, be speaking with another introvert!

I'm happy to report that Sonya did respond to Tyler's message, and they continued to chat and then met up a few times. Although this exercise won't get a response *every time*, it does help you stand out and use your strength of meaningful and intentional conversation to find a better match.

Scene Two: Bombarded!

Khalid often received feedback from dates that in conversations, they felt "bombarded with questions." People said it was hard to engage in conversation with Khalid. This left him feeling more anxious in social situations, and he did not get second or third dates.

I needed to know just what Khalid was doing, but I couldn't ask him to record his dates and I couldn't follow him around. So I asked if Khalid had any text conversations that might be an example of what others were saying. Khalid showed me an exchange he'd had after a first date.

Tues 10:03 a.m.

Khalid: Hey!! I'm so glad we got to meet! I had a really great time! It's cool that you're into woodworking and welding! Me too! What are you currently working on? Have you been to the new shop they opened up in town??

Tues 1:12 p.m.

Khalid: I hope you're having a good day! I just checked out that pizza place you told me about. You're right! Great Hawaiian pizza! How did you find this place? Thanks for telling me about it!

Tues 2:23 p.m.

Alex: Hi! It was nice meeting you too. Yeah, I'm working on a project at my house. I'm going to start working from home so I'm expanding my workspace area. I've been working on that all day, actually. So glad you liked the pizza place! Hands down the best Hawaiian there is!

Continued ››

> *Tues 2:45 p.m.*
>
> Khalid: Oh!! Workspace expansion! So cool! What are you doing? New bookshelves? Bigger desk space? You should totally get a dual monitor system. I can help with that too! And lighting! Definitely need good lighting for video calls. Do you have a lot of video calls? I know someone who could help you with that if you need it.
>
> *Tues 7:39 p.m.*
>
> Khalid: I hope you had a good day!
>
> *Tues 8:53 p.m.*
>
> Alex: Listen, I really like you and you seem pretty cool. I have a lot going on and it's hard to respond to messages throughout the day. Maybe we can chat later or meet up later this week to talk more?

Let's Break It Down

Khalid was an introvert trying to fit into an extroverted world by using small talk. Unfortunately, Khalid was not very good at it. What I read from Khalid's texts with Alex (and could assume was happening in person, too) was Khalid trying too hard to compensate for what he felt was not being social enough or too quiet.

By nature, Khalid was not chatty, though he had received messages throughout his life that chatting helped people fit in at work and in social situations. So when he was struggling with dating, he tried to chitchat with others. Because this was not a natural behavior for him, it caused a lot of social anxiety, which only made things worse. As Khalid reported, dates would either ghost him or ask for distance to alleviate their own discomfort at Khalid's conversation bombardment and too much connection early in the relationship.

PUT IT IN PLAY

"It seems like you really want to connect with others," I said after reading Khalid's chat conversation.

"Yeah! I do," he confirmed.

"If we're being honest, I have an idea as to why your dates aren't working out. What if your attempt to connect and fit in is coming across as intrusive or overwhelming? I wonder if we could slow things down a bit and learn to balance your skill set of deep conversation with a little bit of small talk."

I walked Khalid through the text conversation with Alex to explore alternative ways the conversation could have gone. Khalid highlighted what I had suspected, which is that he was already anxious this date wouldn't work out. Anxiety will show up where it's least appreciated, and others will inevitably pick up on this. Naturally and unintentionally, humans steer away from uncomfortable situations and behaviors, and Khalid's anxiety was becoming a subtle turnoff. So the first tip I had for him was to manage his anxiety. I taught Khalid several anxiety management techniques and encouraged him to practice daily, especially before a date. Here are other tips Khalid and I discussed.

Less is more when it comes to asking questions. A thoughtful question can be like a dopamine hit that rewards the brain for something new to think about and can make you and your date want to talk more. However, too much at one time can be overstimulating or hard to organize, which can lead to the recipient shutting down.

Silence is golden. Although our modern age is all about instant gratification and endless input, keep in mind that some people may not be on their phones 24/7. As Alex said, he had been busy all day and came back to a flood of messages from Khalid. Just as too many questions can be overstimulating, too many messages can also be overwhelming. Think about what it's like for you to get flooded with too much stimulation.

Say it out loud or role-play. I use this technique all the time with clients. If you want to know how something you say will be received, have someone else say it to you first. For Khalid, I simply repeated to him what he said in all his texts, and he understood how Alex may have felt on the other end. Alternatively, if you don't have a friend to help you role-play, you can say it aloud to yourself.

Stick with open-ended questions. Those are questions that can't be answered with a yes, no, or some other very simple answer. Open-ended questions allow for conversation to continue to flow, whereas closed questions can easily end a conversation. Khalid asking Alex, "How did you find this place?" was a great open-ended question. It allowed Alex to share more about their interests, which could lead to further and deeper conversation.

REFLECT ON IT

For most of your life, you probably received similar messages to the ones Khalid and Tyler heard about engaging in conversation with others. Some of these messages might have created limiting beliefs about yourself, as we discussed in chapter 3. They likely also have created more anxiety for you.

Think about your natural ability to make meaningful conversation. Using positive statements, how would you describe your conversation ability? "I am concise and to the point," or, "I tell others what's on my mind" are a couple of examples. What else can you think of?

When you think about your style of conversation using these positive statements, how does that make you feel, compared to when others tell you that your conversation style is a weakness or deficit? Here are few words to help you out:

→ Empowered   → Direct

→ Confident   → Skilled

→ Knowledgeable   → Able

→ Clear

Finally, think about starting a conversation with these words or positive statements in mind. How might you start that conversation differently now?

Chapter 8

Deep and Meaningful

As an introvert, it's likely you prefer to have
fewer but deeper and more meaningful connections
with others. Those connections take time and energy
to form. At times, it can feel like a double-edged sword,
tending to your introverted energy needs while building
a relationship that works for you. You may find yourself exhausted juggling the different areas of your life,
including dating. How often have you tried to change
your dating habits and still not found a meaningful
connection? This leads to more frustration with dating
and, potentially, giving up on it. Let's look at how other
introverts have used their desire for deeper connections
to make dating work in their favor.

Scene One: Club Deflated

In chapter 4, you met Paul, who was starting to have more success
dating after better understanding his values and needs. He had even
begun pushing himself out of his comfort zone by trying to meet
people in social situations. However, a few months after our initial

session, he looked rather distressed and began telling me about a singles night he had gone to with his friends at a bar on the weekend.

"At first, I was really excited," he said. "The beginning of the night was fun. I met some new people, and we had decent conversations. Then more people started showing up, and it got louder and more crowded."

"How did you feel at that point?" I asked.

"I started to feel less engaged," he replied, "so I went off into a quieter side room to keep chatting with the guys I had met. Though people just kept coming there, too. After a while, it was hard to focus and I stopped having fun." He seemed quite deflated.

"That sounds like a really stimulating place," I said, silently thinking I would feel overwhelmed there, too!

"Yes, it kind of was, as more people got there. It wasn't bad at first, though. I really want to meet someone, and it seems that's what people were doing that night."

Before I could say anything else, Paul continued, "Nothing was wrong. It just feels like something was missing. I met some interesting people, but I just wasn't happy afterward." He looked even more deflated and slumped lower into the couch.

"It sounds like you're trying to combine your social life and your romantic life, and it's not balancing," I said. "What would it be like if you kept your friend activities separate from dating? Once you form a connection or relationship with a guy, then you could begin to merge them a bit more."

Let's Break It Down

Although Paul was becoming more aware of his needs, including his need for deeper connections, I noticed he was still following the same patterns of trying to meet guys in overstimulating or crowded environments where superficial connections and small talk were more common than intellectual conversations.

Clubs were common meeting places for Paul's peer group, and I could understand his desire to go where his friends went. However, I also knew this was not the best setting for him to make a deep connection with someone he might want to date. Once the relationship was established, then I could see Paul better enjoying these social clubs without the added anxiety and stimulation of trying to meet someone in a loud and crowded place.

After chatting with Paul about this repeating pattern, he disclosed that he struggled balancing "friend time" with "dating time." He was trying to do both at once, although this was not the best way for him to meet someone to date and form a deep connection with.

Dating, like a lot of things in life, can take up a lot of time! Paul's plan to spend time with friends and try to meet people to date all at once is common for a lot of my clients. However, it's not always the best plan of action when you are trying to balance two different parts of your life, and a lively social setting may be okay for friend time but not for dating time. Think about it: If you planned a date with someone, you wouldn't tell your friends to show up at the same time and place and try to run back and forth between them, would you?

PUT IT IN PLAY

It's common for introverts to experience dating burnout if they are making a lot of superficial connections but not forging more meaningful and fulfilling bonds. I encourage clients to make time for dating each day or week, but also to set boundaries. Dating, in general, can be pretty intrusive, with the influx of messages and a need to respond or the amount of time it takes each week to meet people, and this can lead to feeling overwhelmed. And that can lead to dating dissatisfaction, jumping on and off the dating apps, or just stopping all together.

Here are some ideas for how to prevent dating burnout.

→ **Dedicate a specific amount of time each week to dating.** This can include when and how often to use dating apps or send messages, as well as how often you want to go on dates and for what length of time.

→ **Decide how many people you want to chat with or meet at a time.** For someone who loses energy interacting with others, this is a really important tip. The more people you chat with or meet, the more energy you're losing and the more recharge time you'll need.

→ **Seek out people you are genuinely interested in.** While an extrovert may be content to make chitchat and flirt on a date with someone they don't have a lot in common with, this is far less true for introverts. However, exchanging real, honest thoughts during meaningful interactions can actually energize an introvert rather than drain their internal battery. The key here is to seek out people you find interesting and who find you interesting in return, rather than rolling the dice on somebody you don't click with.

→ **Pick just one or two dating apps to use at a time.** The more dating apps you have, the more time you'll need to send or respond to messages.

→ **Keep chats in the app until the first date is set.** I borrowed this tip from dating coach Erika Ettin, who owns the dating service Just a Little Nudge. This also helps manage who you are talking with and prevents dating from intruding into other areas of your life, such as social time or work time. A cousin of mine once said he would dedicate a separate phone number to dating. If moving chats outside the app is your prefer- ence, then consider getting a free phone number or chat app just for dating chats.

→ **Make a list of three to five places you are comfortable going to.** The more comfortable you are with the location, the more comfortable you'll feel about meeting a new person. When the topic of meeting comes up, let the other person know your preferences and stick to them.

→ **Think of at least one or two places or groups where you could go to meet potential dates IRL.** Although dating apps are convenient, in-person interactions provide a different experience of meeting someone. For some, IRL leads to a better dating experience, including more chances of going on actual dates. We'll explore dating in real-life situations more in chapter 11.

Scene Two: Keeping It Deep

Nina and Hans had been dating for a year when they decided to move in together. Before that, Nina described the budding relationship as enjoyable, relaxing, and pressure-free. She and Hans set aside specific times each week for date nights and would often stay together one to two nights a week. She had enough time for herself and her hobbies, and they didn't interfere with her relationship with Hans. One of Nina's favorite regular dates with Hans was when they attended open mic poetry night at their local coffee shop. She particularly enjoyed discussing the readings the next day over brunch at their favorite café.

After a few months of living together, Nina noticed changes in the relationship, including more superficial daily conversation such as, "How are you?" and, "How was your day at work?" and a decrease in the amount of time she and Hans spent each week in deep conversation and closer connection. She also noticed fewer date nights to the coffee shop or next-day brunch. On the upside, Nina did notice that their daily routines didn't change much, such as spending time on their separate hobbies or binging a TV show as part of self-care.

Nina talked to a few of her friends who had also started getting more serious with their partners, including living together. She was relieved to find that others were experiencing similar changes in their relationships and that she wasn't alone. What she also noticed is that these similar concerns occurred more often with her friends who were cohabitating and less with friends who still lived apart from their partners.

Let's Break It Down

What Nina and her friends experienced is the change in relationships when partners begin to live together. Dating forces you, in a good way, to make your relationship and time with your partner a priority. Deep connections don't form overnight, and they can't be rushed. Introverts typically prefer deeper relationships and are pretty good at making deep connections. However, once they are formed, both partners must keep working to maintain them.

A relationship naturally starts with the excitement of dating, where you prioritize time and plans with your partner. As the relationship progresses, such as moving in with each other or making plans for the future, it's natural to begin to integrate your lives in ways such as merging your daily routine, creating expectations for roles within the relationship, and maintaining some personal time for hobbies or friendships.

Living together makes spending time together easier and builds on the bond already established while dating. Proximity also allows you to get into daily relationship routines, which are necessary for the relationship to grow. During this adjustment period, prioritizing your relationship may unintentionally fall by the wayside. That happens a lot.

When you are around someone more often, it's natural for the dynamic to change. You can still have the deep connection you experienced in dating and also make some room for more superficial experiences that help hold the relationship together.

Keep your connection alive. While establishing your new routine with your partner, don't forget to prioritize relationship time. Be sure to schedule regular date nights, just as you did while dating.

Keep doing new things. As part of your regular date nights, be sure to find new things to do with each other! What different activities and experiences can keep the excitement and passion going? One activity I give clients is to create a date jar. You can start by writing down activities or places you want to check out or visit. When you come across something, write it down and put it in the date jar. Every couple of weeks, pull out a slip of paper and, voilà, a new date idea!

Maintain passion in your relationship. Without passion— which can be both emotional and physical—a relationship can become more like a platonic friendship. Passion is maintained through newness plus attraction. The metaphor I can offer is food. When a restaurant offers a new menu item for a limited time, we get all excited and really want to try it. You may feel a new attraction for a restaurant that you've been to hundreds of times. When the newness wears off, your attraction decreases and you stop going—until there is another new item on the menu. Relationships need to have something new to keep them alive and exciting. This could be doing a new activity, visiting a new place, or changing up your appearance with a new outfit or hairstyle.

Embrace familiarity. For relationships to last, they also need a sense of security and stability. Living with a partner allows this to develop. Find ways to embrace the mundane parts of the relationship, such as the routine chores or after-work greetings. Create a special thing that you and your partner do for each other in the morning or after work, such as leaving funny notes in their bag to find at work or having deep conversations while doing the dishes together.

REFLECT ON IT

Using the introvert's natural abilities and skills, you can create deeper connections while dating and as your relationship progresses. Along the way, we discussed setting boundaries to prevent frustration and overstimulation with dating, as well as learning how to keep that deep connection alive once your relationship progresses.

After reading these sections, ask yourself:

→ How do I form deeper connections with others?

→ Do I accept myself for who I am and show others my true self, or am I trying to show them a person I'm not?

→ Do I need to set any specific boundaries with dating? How could this help me form more authentic relationships?

Chapter 9

The Strength of Silence and Solitude

You know that old adage "Silence is golden"? Well, I'm here to tell you that silence can be many other things as well, including intriguing and alluring—which can make dating fun for introverts and enhance relationships. Extroverts often fill any quiet space with words and sounds. Introverts can not only embrace the silence but enjoy it *and* can use this silence to their advantage, especially at the beginning of a relationship. In this chapter, we'll look at how you can lean into well-placed quietude while dating, rather than trying to keep up with talkative partners. We'll also look at the role of solitude when a relationship begins to form, and how you can balance it with interaction.

Scene One: Be Where You Are

Although it was her fourth date with Toni, Michelle found herself especially nervous tonight. Her bed looked like her closet had exploded as she tried on outfit after outfit and finally decided on a simple dress and cardigan. Michelle was beginning to think she needed to fill all the quiet space on their dates with conversation or else Toni might think she was aloof or disinterested, but she didn't want to just blurt out answers.

The whole time she was getting ready, she thought, "What are we going to talk about? My week was boring. Toni's not going to find me interesting or exciting. I should take a list of questions. Yes! That will help fill the space." Michelle began to Google topics to discuss on her date.

Michelle got to the café early to prepare for the conversation. When she realized she had 30 minutes until Toni would arrive, she began to feel a bit awkward sitting alone and feeling so anxious about the date. She found herself playing with the scarf tied to her bag handle and realized how relaxing it felt. She also noticed the café's décor, which she hadn't noticed when she arrived, and took in the fabulous smells of coffee and baked goods.

Becoming lost in her thoughts, Michelle recalled her therapist discussing how silence can be useful when chatting with others. They discussed Michelle's tendency to take a few beats to respond, because she liked to reflect and show genuine interest and connection. She also recalled how they discussed that blurting out answers or interjecting could come across as more awkward than taking one's time to respond. She remembered her therapist's tip to take a deep breath before responding, so she wouldn't rush.

"Hi, Michelle!" Toni said, walking up and pulling her out of her thoughts.

"Hi!" Michelle responded with a huge smile and feeling much calmer now.

"I hope you haven't been here too long," Toni said.

"Oh no! Just a few minutes to grab us a good table," Michelle replied, secretly laughing at herself. "Tell me, how did your project work out last week?"

"So glad you asked! I was able to get the supplies to …" Toni began as Michelle sat silently showing interest and listening to the story without feeling any need to interject.

Let's Break It Down

Silence can be a double-edged sword for the introvert. Of course, quietly staring into space for minutes at a time won't get you very far on a date. But what if Michelle leaned into the gaps between talking, rather than pressuring herself to fill them with whatever popped into her mind?

The in-between parts of a conversation are when introverts process information and formulate a response. If you're on a date with someone who talks at a faster pace than you, it's easy to worry that they may interpret you as aloof, distant, or bored. In truth, though, leaning into the pauses between words can convey calm composure—even mystery and intrigue.

On her date, Michelle made the mistake of projecting her worries onto the situation, rather than staying centered in the present. If some well-placed moments of silence are truly an issue for your date—and they are unwilling to meet you halfway—chances are you may not be the most compatible couple. That said, if you have a quieter demeanor, it's important to change the narrative in your head. When you can embrace rather than reject your natural quiet, you can stay engaged while getting to know someone and better connect with them.

PUT IT IN PLAY

Embracing silence doesn't always come easy, but when you can see it as a virtue rather than a setback, it can transform how you interact with others, including on dates.

Remember, nonverbal communication is real communication. It's often said that a picture is worth a thousand words. In the same way, our interactions with others are about much more than what's said. Eye contact, smiling, posture, and gestures greatly influence our ability to connect with others. You can see a powerful example of this in the documentary *The Artist Is Present*. In it, the performance artist Marina Abramović sits for hours across from any museum guest at New York's Museum of Modern Art who wanted to sit in front of her without talking. At one point, her former lover, Ulay, whom she had not seen in more than two decades, sat in front of her. They only sat for a minute or so before he left. Without either saying any words, the viewer can see them both experience a wide range of emotions, with changing gestures and facial expressions, including smiles and tears. This silent interaction shows more emotional connection and feelings than words ever could.

Try eye-gazing. Eye-gazing—sitting and connecting without words—is often used by therapists to help clients work through the discomfort of silently looking into another's eyes, as well as to help couples create new connections that aren't physical or verbal. At times, words can be distracting. Many people will use words like "um" or "and" to fill a quiet space or avoid discomfort. However, when you break through and get comfortable with silence, you can truly appreciate that connection is about much more than what you say. While this is a great activity to do with an established lover, it's obviously not a first-date activity. I suggest trying this with a close friend or family member who you don't feel self-conscious around.

Charge your internal battery with some quiet time before a date. As you know, introverts tend to be energized by their internal world of emotions, ideas, and impressions and drained by social interactions. Gathering energy isn't always easy, especially amid the noise of modern living. It takes time for introverts to charge their batteries, and they can be depleted faster than those of extroverts.

On the evening before a date, or the day of, carve out time for solitude to charge your energy reserves. You can go for a solo walk, read a book, meditate, or do anything else that lets you lean into quiet, so you'll have more energy for chatting later. Try not to schedule dates immediately after situations where you'll have to talk a lot, like a get-together with friends or back-to-back meetings at work.

Stay in the present. Rather than worrying about how your silence is being perceived, center yourself in the present moment. A great way to do this is to take a few seconds to experience the moment with your senses. Notice what you can hear, smell, and see right now. If you mind starts to wander, bring it back to the sensations of the moment. You can also stay present through touch. If you often get anxious on dates, take a small, inconspicuous object, such as a keychain or a smooth stone, to keep near you. Hold it or touch it when you're anxious to bring yourself back to the present and help calm your nerves. Do certain smells soothe you? Spray your token with a calming essential oil, too.

Scene Two: The Friend Zone

Leigh and Adrian came to see me because they were constantly fighting and said they were having trouble communicating. As I was getting to know them a bit more, I learned that they met while volunteering with a local animal shelter a couple of years earlier. They didn't start dating until a year or so after meeting. "We never really talked to each other when we were working, other than a cordial greeting," Leigh reported.

They got to know each other better one day while they were both out walking dogs. Then they connected again at a large fundraising event and realized they shared an interest in the cause it was promoting. "After that, we continued chatting every few days and meeting up for coffee or game nights," Leigh said. "It's like our relationship just formed without intention."

"So, what seems to be the problem now?" I asked.

They both looked at each other before Adrian said, "Well, we really like each other, but we just feel like friends and we only do 'friend things' and not 'relationship things,' if you get what I'm saying."

"It sounds like you're saying you're not intimate with each other; is that correct? You both feel like you're in the friend zone?" I asked, making sure I understood them. They both emphatically shook their heads.

I continued to ask more questions to find out more about Leigh and Adrian's relationship and lifestyle. I discovered that they lived separately, a 20-minute drive apart. They both preferred a lot of alone time and mostly engaged in solo hobbies at home. They both told me they also worked remotely from home in the IT field.

My final question for them: "When or how often do you see each other and talk to each other?"

They both looked at each other and then looked back at me. With a shrug, Leigh responded, "We don't really keep track of that, but maybe a couple of times a week, usually when we catch up with mutual friends."

Let's Break It Down

As we know, introverts enjoy their solitude and are often content being alone. They might not experience the anxiety that an extrovert would if their partner isn't in frequent contact or visiting every few days. However, too much distance or solo time can create issues in a relationship, even between two introverts. These may include:

→ A lack of intimacy, whether emotional or physical; often, couples report feeling more like friends or roommates rather than lovers

→ Not prioritizing the relationship; other areas of life coming before relationship needs

→ Jealousy if the other partner is spending more time with friends or hobbies

→ Feeling insecure about oneself or lower self-esteem related to being a partner who is held at a distance

→ Generally growing apart from each other

Leigh and Adrian didn't find their need for alone time to be a problem and did not feel it negatively affected their general satisfaction with life, but they did find that it was affecting their relationship satisfaction, including their need for physical intimacy and time together. One important thing I heard is that they weren't making time for each other or doing the things they needed to keep their passion alive, which is what separates a romantic relationship from a platonic relationship.

An introvert's need for solitude to rest and recharge is not inherently bad for a relationship. But there is such a thing as too much solitude. It needs to be balanced with plenty of together time with your partner, so that a relationship doesn't start to feel more like a friendship.

PUT IT IN PLAY

Although Adrian and Leigh's problem is a common one for a lot of couples, it's also easily resolved. Couples can restore relationship satisfaction without sacrificing their own needs for alone time.

I often notice that after couples form a solid relationship, they stop dating. That is, they stop going out to restaurants, the movies, bars, vacations, and generally making time to enjoy each other's company. Dating throughout your relationship—whether you're six months together, a year together, or 10-plus years together—helps keep a relationship alive and passionate. Making time for the play aspect of being in a relationship can also lead to intimate desire for the other person. However, there are some things to keep in mind when dating your partner.

Do's

→ Make time to see your partner at least once or twice week.

→ Enjoy shared hobbies or interests.

→ Enjoy interactions with each other that don't involve the distractions of other people or objects (such as computers or cell phones).

→ Share one interesting thing about yourself or your day at least once a day.

→ Set aside time in your day just for yourself and let your partner know about it.

→ Purchase a set of conversation cards from an online retailer and see what you learn about each other. (Check out my suggestions in the Resources section, page 167.)

→ Create time and space for intimacy, even if you have to plan a specific date for intimate time.

Don'ts

→ Talk about the relationship "laundry list," such as your disagreements, finances, or household chores.

→ Talk about other people, such as friends or family.

→ Double-book yourself so that your attention is taken away from your partner or the relationship.

→ Skip date nights or planned time together. Reschedule if something important comes up.

→ Think that too much distance in your relationship is one-sided; it always takes two to maintain a relationship.

REFLECT ON IT

Hopefully this chapter has helped you appreciate the virtues of quieter moments when dating. As you've learned, leaning into the pauses between words can convey composure, mystery, and even intrigue.

When it comes to relationships, you can and should enjoy quiet time to recharge, just so long as this doesn't get in the way of quality time with your partner. As an introvert, you may need to stay on top of this to help maintain the fun and spark in a relationship. Try reflecting on the following questions to think through how you can best achieve this.

→ Thinking about silence and emotional distance in my relationships or dating experiences, what comes up for me when I experience either of these? Do I feel discomfort and disconnected or do I feel peace and calmness? Would my dates or partners say the same?

→ How has emotional distance affected my dating or relationship experiences? Was there too much or too little distance? Does this create dating and relationship distress for me?

→ Reviewing the suggestions for do's and don'ts in this chapter, how might my dating experience or relationships be different if I tried these?

Part Three

Troubleshooting for Single Introverts

Now that you have a better understanding of the strengths and challenges of being an introvert, in this final part of the book we'll troubleshoot some common dating issues that single introverts often face. We'll examine some typical scenarios of meeting, attracting, and interacting with dates, as well as problems that can arise when you're transitioning from dating into a relationship.

Chapter 10

"I Feel Like Online Dating Isn't Right for Me"

Have you been curious to try online dating, but can't bring yourself to dive in? Or perhaps you've already tried it and find it takes up too much of your energy. In this chapter, we'll look at how you can bring your introverted A-game to online dating without feeling out of place or overwhelmed.

Here's the Story

Juan was single after the end of a long-term relationship, and after some time alone, they were ready to date again. When they left the dating pool well over a decade ago, online dating wasn't really a thing. In fact, there was still a stigma attached to having met a person online. Now, according to a 2019 study, couples are more likely to meet a romantic partner online than through personal contacts and connections. Not only has the stigma disappeared, but the technology has improved, too, making it easier to use.

Still, when returning to the dating scene, Juan felt it had become a lot more overwhelming than it used to be. They responded with an emphatic "No" when I mentioned trying a dating app. I asked them about their reservations.

"It just seems so intrusive and fake," they explained. "Do people actually read profiles or do they just match with dozens of people until someone messages them?"

"Have you ever tried an app?" I asked.

With slight hesitation, as if I had just caught them stealing a cookie, they said, "Well . . . no. I mean, I've downloaded a couple on my phone. I did open them, but I felt uneasy having to share so much information and put pictures up. Do they want my fingerprints, too?" they asked sarcastically.

"Yes, the apps can be overwhelming, and creating a profile is time-consuming and does ask for a lot of info about you. I get it if you're not willing to share your fingerprints just yet with a stranger," I added with a friendly smile. "But what might it be like if you started with just one app? And what if you already knew what information to share before creating a profile?"

Let's Break It Down

Juan's initial experience with dating apps sounded similar to someone's first experience at a Las Vegas casino, with all the bright lights, loud noises, and different people wanting different things. For introverts, the sheer variety of dating apps and sites—including Tinder, Bumble, Match, OkCupid, Hinge, and many more—can feel overwhelming.

Then there's the need to share personal information on your profile, which, for an introvert who enjoys spending time in their private inner world, can feel like an intrusion. You may start writing about yourself but abandon ship when it starts to feel like you need to compose something longer than the Declaration of Independence.

As I suggested to Juan, it's helpful to first think of three to five facts to share about yourself, rather than feeling pressure to craft a complete picture of who you are. This gives you more control over *what* and *how much* information you share, without it feeling as if you are being forced to reveal too much. This also means that potential dates have something more meaningful to talk to you about, rather than launching into tedious and energy-draining chitchat.

Joining one app at a time is also helpful. Even though the same profile can be used across several apps, trying to set up more than one account or sharing your private information several times in a row could be an emotional drain. One app at a time lets you test the waters and begin to chat with (or meet) others without the additional maintenance work.

PUT IT IN PLAY

Whether you have yet to set up a profile or are struggling to click with people you're chatting with, here are some useful tips for intro-verts to make online dating work for you instead of you working for online dating.

Tips for Setting Up Your Profile

For those who are still hesitant or concerned about the process or shar-ing information, here are a few things to consider when you're starting on your profile.

Be authentic. Don't try to present yourself as someone you're not. Show your true self in your profile, not who you think you should be, including an extrovert. People will pick up on the fakeness and inauthenticity. Maybe you're a massive gamer, caring for a family of 36 houseplants, or a prize-winning line dancer. Whatever makes you tick, by sharing your passions, you're more likely to attract someone who appreciates you for you. This extends to the photos you post on your profile, too. Don't feel like you need to post the most flattering shots. Authenticity is attractive, and a picture showing a genuine smile or an unplanned moment is likely to showcase your true personality much more than the "perfect" posed shot.

Describe yourself so others see you in a positive and intriguing way. Do you want others to see you as timid and shy or as thoughtful and well-spoken? Do you describe yourself as "obsessed with . . ." or as an avid learner of new things? Think about the reasons you want a person to be intrigued enough to talk with you and write about those qualities.

Have a friend read your profile and give feedback. Friends will read from an outside perspective and share how another person will view your profile. They can point out when something sounds flattering or when something doesn't sound like you. They might also point out traits or characteristics that you didn't consider.

Tips for Making the Right Connections

If you can get over the initial hurdles to setting up a profile, there is a lot of natural appeal for introverts when it comes to online dating. Rather than making small talk at crowded parties or shouting over music at bars, you can browse potential matches from the comfort of your sofa and take as much time as you need to craft messages to people who catch your fancy.

Still, many find that, rather than being a useful tool for limiting energy-draining interactions with too many people, apps can result in lots of small talk that leads nowhere. Let's look at some useful tips when it comes to making the right types of connections.

Some things bear repeating: Be authentic! This extends to when you start making contact with others and chatting with them. Don't feel like you need to bend to someone else's interests or opinions to attract them to you. You'll just end up wasting your time and energy.

Tap into your listening skills. Whether in person or through chats, use your introvert listening skills to your advantage. Your date may have had a frustrating day and feel comfortable sharing with you. (That's a step closer to a connection!) Take the time to hear or read what they are saying and respond with empathy or understanding.

The early bird gets the worm (or date). Many of us, especially women, have learned to sit back and let the other person initiate. But modern dating has very few rules for how to start a date. Also, just because you like someone doesn't mean they get an instant notification, unlike when you send them a message. If you're really interested in a person, send a message with a personal opening line, such as what you liked about their profile or discussing a common interest.

REFLECT ON IT

After reading this chapter about how you can make online dating work for you, consider these next steps for making better online connections.

→ What three to five facts would you like to share with a stranger? If you currently have a dating profile, see if those facts are listed.

→ Write out a draft of your profile or review your existing one. When you read it back to yourself, does it sound authentic? If not, what can you add or remove to create more authenticity?

→ Have a friend read your profile to ensure it's meeting your goals for dating.

If you find yourself losing motivation in a sea of matches and small talk online, feel free to take a week or so off the apps to recharge your battery. Use the time to consider how you can prioritize speaking with people you are genuinely interested in, rather than those who may only be superficially appealing—for their looks or something else that doesn't speak to your core values.

Chapter 11

"I Find It Hard to Meet People in Real Life"

While dating apps may provide some advan-tages for introverts, that doesn't mean you have to rule out meeting people in real-life situations. Many introverts feel they are at a disadvantage when it comes to meeting people in a more spontaneous way, given their disinclination for socializing. However, as we'll explore in this chapter, it's more than possible to stay true to yourself while meeting people IRL—and enjoy yourself along the way!

Here's the Story

Wes was a recent college graduate who had just moved to a much bigger city for a job and now found himself in a new place without any local friends. His job kept him pretty busy as he learned his tasks, got acquainted with coworkers, and attended daily work meetings. For the first few weeks, he found himself emotionally and physically exhausted from the new job and just wanted to spend his free time at home reading, binge-watching the latest anime, or gaming with his online friends.

Several of his coworkers were also single (though not his type and vice versa), and one day at work a few of them were chatting about a new speed dating event being held at a popular bar around the corner from the office next Thursday. The event was free, with a cash bar.

"This sounds great!" said Mindy, one of his coworkers, and immediately RSVP'd for the event. Two other coworkers also signed up. "Come on, Wes! It'll be fun!" Mindy said. Her intention was to be encouraging, although Wes was actually feeling pressured to go because he didn't socialize much with his new coworkers.

"Fine, fine. I'll give it a try. What's the worst that can happen, other than that I go home without a date, right?" Wes felt anxious about what he was signing up for, though. Speed dating was not exactly his speed.

After work on Thursday, everyone headed to the bar and signed in for the speed dating event. They pushed their way to the bar to get drinks. A lot of people had showed up, so Wes was sardined between his coworkers and a bunch of strangers. While he was waiting, he attempted to chat with a petite brunette standing next to him. "Hey there," he said, trying to get her attention. When she didn't seem to hear him above the noise of so many conversations, he tried to move closer, lost his balance, and almost fell on top of her. She glared at him with irritation as he profusely apologized. "Not the best start to convincing strangers to date me," Wes thought.

He sat down at the speed dating table and listened to the instructions for the event. He would have five minutes to chat with the person in front of him before a timer went off indicating it was time to switch. The event was 30 minutes total and he'd get to chat with six people. "This doesn't sound too bad," he thought. At least he wouldn't have to struggle to be noticed and heard above everyone else in the crowded bar.

But when the dating began, Wes didn't know how to start quick conversations. If the person sitting across from him didn't speak first, they just sat in awkward silence. He was pretty sure four minutes went by before one conversation got started. When he tried to start conversations, he found himself asking, "Do you come to things like this a lot?" which sounded like the cheesiest line ever.

By his fourth date and 20 minutes in, Wes was just wishing this would end and he could go home and be alone. While trying to be attentive to the person in front of him, he was also looking for his coworkers and saw Mindy laughing away with her current date. When the last buzzer went off, Wes snuck out of the bar and headed for home, convinced he would be single forever.

Let's Break It Down

A common trap many introverts find with meeting people in real life is that most events and situations are geared for the extrovert, who might be energized by a fast-paced, stimulating setting. These situations require you to quickly come up with questions and responses and offer little time to process your thoughts. As we've already discussed, introverts often do best in quiet places where they have plenty of time to process information. When you only have a moment to chat with someone and make a connection, introverts often do not shine.

As Wes found, when you're trying to meet people IRL, you might also get into a situation where you're uncomfortably squeezed between people who are having their own conversations or need to move around from person to person and spot to spot. But introverts typically feel more comfortable when they can find one spot to settle in, ease into conversation, and connect. You already embrace your preference for slow and careful consideration in other areas of your life, so why not in dating, too? Introverts don't have to meet others in real life the same way extroverts do.

Rather than being pressured into situations where you know you will be uncomfortable and can't put your best foot forward, think about how you can meet others in real life in settings that feel more comfortable for you. There are many ways introverts can stay true to themselves, preserve their energy, and have fun meeting people IRL.

Ideas for Meeting People IRL

The advantage of meeting someone with a shared interest is that you already have something in common and can skip the awkwardness of a blind date or trying to find something to do with a stranger. As an introvert, by doing something that interests you, rather than attending events for the sole purpose of finding a date, you are more likely to feel engaged and energized rather than exhausted. Here are some great ways to meet people IRL. (In the next chapter, we'll look at how to improve your small talk when meeting people in real life.)

→ **Take a class.** Have you been meaning to improve on your broken high school French? Perhaps you've always been interested in mastering Mexican cooking. Whatever it is, taking a class is a great way to improve yourself while also meeting others in a low-pressure environment.

→ **Volunteer for a cause you care about.** Whether it's at your local animal shelter or community garden, volunteering can be a great way to meet someone who shares your interests and aligns with your values.

→ **Host a dinner party or barbecue and have your friends invite a single friend.** This is another nonintimidating way to meet new people. Having your friends around means you don't have to talk only to strangers, plus having a mutual friend means you already have something in common.

→ **Get outdoors.** Whether it's a hiking group, a running club, or a weekly meditation or yoga meetup in the park, heading outdoors is a great way to meet like-minded folks without having to make conversation over loud music at boozy bars or clubs.

How to Preserve Your Energy Dating IRL

Keep dates low key and short. Earlier in this book, I encouraged you to create a list of first-date places. I also suggest keeping these places low key—spots with less going on that are less likely to be crowded. Also, keep the dates short and choose a place that will support a short date. Coffee or a drink after work could be short dates, or not so short. You can decide how fast to finish your beverage, depending on how it's going.

Don't schedule dates for days when you are already socializing. If you meet your date on a day you've spent socializing with friends, family, or coworkers, you're already exhausted and probably not looking forward to the date. You may also project your tiredness while on the date and not be your best self.

Don't date too many people at once, but don't feel you need to date just one person, either. Too many people can lead to dating burnout. Too few people can lead to a one-sided experience if the other person is dating others and dividing their time and energy when you aren't. This may lead to you feeling hurt and defeated when the relationship ends before progressing to something more. I can't tell you an exact number, as each person is different. I do suggest trying to date two or three people and see how that goes.

REFLECT ON IT

If meeting people in real life has felt like a chore or filled you with anxiety, now is the time to challenge your misconceptions that IRL dating isn't suited to introverts.

→ Reflect on how it would feel to take the pressure off yourself when it comes to meeting people in real-life situations. Just because you may not be the life of the party doesn't mean you can't enjoy low-pressure social settings with like-minded people.

→ Remember, it's okay to plan short-and-sweet dates. This allows you to preserve your energy, focus on a few topics of conversation, and get a sense of the other person without having to hang around if you're just not feeling a spark.

→ This week, try signing up for a class or a group activity where you can meet others. You can refer to the ideas earlier in this chapter for inspiration, or get creative thinking of ways to meet like-minded people who share your interests.

→ When it comes to meeting new people, what tips from this chapter can you implement to make sure you preserve your energy and enjoy yourself?

Chapter 12

"I Need to Make Small Talk, but I Don't Want to Be Fake"

By now, we know that introverts tend to prefer deep connections with others, including in conversation. Instead of sitting and chatting about the weather or traffic delays, you may be more happy sitting in silence in the company of another person. However, dating does require some small talk, as this is the gateway to a deeper conversation and connection.

Here's the Story

Kiera was headed out for her second date of the week. She was already nervous, as her last date had felt like a disaster. When she arrived for that date, it seemed as if they sat for five minutes in silence before Kiera asked about Jin's day. Jin answered, "Not too bad," which didn't lead to any other conversation. Not really interested in Jin's plans and feeling like she was prying into his life, Kiera forced herself to ask what he was doing that weekend, and she continued to receive short, closed-ended answers. After another awkward 10 minutes to finish her iced coffee, Kiera politely ended the date by saying she had to get back to work.

Now it was a few days later. Taking deep breaths, Kiera walked up to the corner café and was relieved to see only a few people were seated inside. It was a hot day, so she didn't want to sit outside, but she also didn't want to get overwhelmed with too much noise from others' conversations. Kiera recognized Hayley from her profile photo and walked up smiling. Kiera had read up on small talk after the disastrous date with Jin and tried a few tips she learned. "Hey Hayley, I'm Kiera. It's nice to finally meet you in person. How do you feel about sitting inside, because we're having a crazy heat wave today?"

"Hi! I'm glad to meet you, too. Yes, inside works for me. I can't believe it's so hot in March."

The two grabbed a table inside and ordered. Kiera remembered Hayley's profile said she had recently moved to the area. "I believe you're new to the area? Where did you move from?"

"I am. I moved here three months ago from Cincinnati. My job offered a promotion that I couldn't turn down."

"That's exciting for you." Kiera made sure her voice and body language showed enthusiasm for Hayley's success. She wondered whether she should ask more about Hayley's new job or her life in Cincinnati. She felt her body temperature rising with nervousness and she began to fidget.

With the awkward silence, Hayley interjected, "So, did you grow up in this area?"

"I did," Kiera responded, internally kicking herself for creating an awkward moment and not elaborating on the answer.

The two finished their lunch with more small talk and some awkward silence between each question. They parted ways with Kiera feeling upset because the date seemed to start out so well, but she wasn't sure if Hayley would be interested in another date.

Let's Break It Down

As we saw with Kiera and Jin, you might struggle to connect in conversation when you're really not interested in superficial topics. You may feel insincere and that you're faking interest. I think it's important to understand that small talk does not always equate to fakeness. Small talk might *feel* inauthentic due to your own discomfort and the fact that the conversation is not very deep.

Also remember that what constitutes small talk is subjective. Yes, there are common small talk topics such as the weather or popular television shows (though, if someone is a meteorologist, then talking about the weather could be substantial for them). It just might not be all that interesting for you. This is when you need to think about balancing creating conversation that works for you and your date.

Some human connection is vital for our mental and physical well-being, and this includes introverts. Small talk can provide this needed connection *and* it can also lead the way to more genuine conversation and connections, as we saw with Kiera and Hayley. In fact, we could look at small talk as the gateway to a less superficial connection. Although Kiera's date with Hayley turned awkward, in hindsight, just meeting and having a conversation allowed both of them to practice their small talk skills and get a dose of human connection.

PUT IT IN PLAY

Chapter 7 discussed how small talk doesn't come naturally for many introverts. Now we'll explore ways you can use small talk to your advantage without feeling fake. If small talk makes you uncomfortable, I suggest practicing with safe people in your life, such as a good friend or a close family member.

Curiosity didn't kill the cat! Most introverts are naturally curious, and you can use this to your advantage when making small talk or to create more substantial conversation. For instance, travel could be a small talk topic, such as, "Do you like to travel?" To take this to the next level, try, "I see you traveled to Peru last year. I love learning about different cultures. What was it like?"

Become a conversation starter. If you're out with an extrovert, you may not need to start the conversation. However, if you're with an introvert, you both might struggle with where to begin or how to carry the conversation. Kiera experienced this with both Jin and Hayley. Practice starting conversations so this becomes more comfortable for you. Have a list of topics about yourself and review the person's profile for topics to ask them about.

Don't jump into the deep end too soon. Don't divulge too much or ask personal questions too soon. I had been chatting with a guy for three weeks when he started telling me about his own therapy work, including medication he was taking, how he was creating change in his life, and what his struggles were. Even as a person who is used to this depth of conversation, it felt too personal too soon. Instead, stick to current goals, such as training for a marathon or buying a new home. This can lead to deeper conversations where you can get to know more about the person.

Be expressive. Body language is also a form of communication. It can express messages such as interest or excitement or ask a question. It can also express the opposite. Once, when watching a video of myself, I remembered the topic being of great interest to me and I was very excited by the conversation. However, I had a blank face with no emotion. *Not* the message I wanted to send! Try having conversations with a friend and ask for feedback on your body language, or watch videos of yourself to see what you may be communicating others.

Go with the flow. Introverts can be prone to overthinking things. As we saw with Kiera, she was doing great with the conversation until her own anxiety stopped her. Either follow-up question would have worked, and she could always ask them both!

REFLECT ON IT

The impersonality of technology sometimes prompts us to ask questions we might not ask a stranger IRL. One rule I encourage clients to keep in mind is whether they would say or ask a stranger this question in the produce section of the supermarket. If you wouldn't say this to a person while examining the tomatoes, rethink whether you would say it in a text. Small talk is beneficial to start a connection, but let's not get too personal before we know if someone prefers Roma tomatoes or cherry tomatoes.

On the other hand, what if you match with someone on an app or get someone's number from your friend's party and your mind goes blank when trying to chat them up? Remind yourself what on their profile or in the conversation attracted you. Was it a photo, a statement, or a shared interest? Send a question or comment about those, such as, "How did you get into mountain biking?" or, "I also love Thai food! Where do you recommend going, and have you tried Vietnamese?" Remember, it's all right if you don't always have something to say, but connection is key to forming a relationship.

Chapter 13

"I Feel Like Flirting Doesn't Come Naturally to Me"

Even though flirting may not be the most important part of dating, it can play a role in creating a spark between you and a date. While some introverts may believe flirting is pointless, fake, or more suited to outgoing extroverts boldly making the moves, as we'll explore in this chapter, a more thoughtful and sincere approach to showing and reciprocating romantic interest gives you an introvert's advantage.

Here's the Story

Junho was getting ready for a party at Niko's house, which, his friend promised him, would be small and not too loud. Plus, there would be several interesting single women to meet. Niko knew Junho was reserved around strangers and had encouraged him to flirt a little more with women he liked, just to show he was interested.

"Flirting is fake and insincere," Junho told Niko emphatically.

"It's only insincere if you are," Niko replied. And that was probably true. Junho had seen plenty of men at bars playfully flirting with women and, often enough, ending up with their phone number. But he preferred direct conversation to smooth talk and casual innuendo. His friends all said he was a good listener and a good conversationalist, too, but that was after he got to know someone. He found it hard to signal his initial interest in a way that seemed natural and genuine.

"Step outside your comfort zone," Niko had told him. And Junho decided tonight he would. He pulled on a pair of skinny jeans and a tailored jacket over a crisp white shirt. Tonight would be different!

Niko's party was as promised—small enough that Junho could have a conversation without screaming. He sat down on the sofa and watched a woman reading tarot cards. One of the men sitting across from her bantered easily and snappily with her. Tonight, Junho wanted to be that guy. So, when a woman wearing big, colorful cat earrings sat down next to him, he said right away, "Well, you look like a cat lover."

"I am," she said. "I have two cats of my own, plus I do some rescue."

"That means you're a kind person. I have a cat, too," Junho said. "And you know what they say about cat guys: sensitive and sweet and sexy." He laughed, and she laughed, too.

"You know, those earrings really suit you," he said. And then Junho leaned across her, supposedly to look at the earrings but really with the idea that he'd lightly brush his hand across her cheek, at which point he knocked her glass of wine into her lap.

"I'm so sorry—" he began, but she was already on her way to the kitchen sink, tossing "It's okay" over her shoulder as she went.

Junho left the party as fast as he could. His mind was racing. "I'm never flirting with anyone again. I'm never going to a party again. I'm never talking to a stranger again . . ."

Let's Break It Down

When we think of flirting, we may imagine dashing extroverts making bold moves or using snappy pickup lines to attract a love interest. While these approaches to flirting may work well in the movies, in real life, an overly forward flirting style can be off-putting. Before we look at how you can embrace a more sincere and subtle flirting style, let's first look at the work of Jeffrey A. Hall, a communication expert from the University of Kansas who specializes in the science of flirting. Hall looked into the flirting habits of more than 10,000 people and grouped them into five flirting styles.

→ **Physical:** This style relies on using body language to indicate sexual interest, be it playing with someone's hair, maintaining eye contact, leaning forward seductively, or a consensual light touch on the arm.

→ **Playful:** This is flirting for fun, without any expectation that it will lead to a sexual connection or a relationship, and includes playful banter and lighthearted jokes.

→ **Polite:** This refers to a more mannered, cautious, and non-sexual approach. People who favor this style of flirting tend to avoid any behavior that could be construed as inappropriate or aggressive.

→ **Sincere:** The sincere flirt prizes emotional connection with a romantic partner and enjoys the getting-to-know-you phase. It can range from offering genuine compliments to displaying interest through active listening and asking follow-up questions.

→ **Traditional:** A step further than polite, this kind of flirting relies on traditional courtship rituals such as bringing flowers on the first date or offering to pay for dinner. Some dates may find these old-fashioned, while others may enjoy the traditions.

So, which styles are best for introverts? If you're more comfortable making meaningful connections, then you may naturally gravitate toward polite and sincere styles of flirting, which both offer some reservation and allow more time for you both to open up to another. Many introverts prefer these styles because they don't require you to be as conventionally outgoing. Reassuringly, Hall's research found that sincere flirting is the most effective when dating.

PUT IT IN PLAY

The style of flirting you use depends on what you're comfortable with and your goal in dating. While a more thoughtful and sincere approach may suit your personality, there's no rule that says introverts can't be playful and respectfully physical on a date to spark some chemistry.

The power of authenticity. Being sincere is a great way for introverts to communicate interest and form an emotional connection. Just make sure your date gets your message! Be sure to offer plenty of genuine compliments and ask well-timed follow-up questions. ("You've led such a fascinating life! What was your time like overseas?") This also plays into the introvert's natural inclination for meaningful conversation rather than superficial chitchat.

It's okay to be subtle. It's totally fine to stick to a more subtle and mannered style of flirting when meeting someone new. In fact, a date may appreciate a slower and more respectful and thoughtful approach. This avoids having to expend lots of your social energy trying to be more outgoing than you may naturally be.

Enjoy yourself. There's no reason you can't lean into playful flirting to express yourself and have fun while connecting to others. The key is to read the room: Use your natural listening and observational skills to make sure your flirting is welcomed and reciprocated.

Use physical cues you are comfortable with. If you aren't particularly comfortable with physical flirting, don't worry. You may gravitate toward more subtle nonverbal cues such as sustained eye contact (though not too long!) or leaning forward toward your date.

REFLECT ON IT

You've probably read articles encouraging you to ask "why" questions to show interest in what someone is saying. However, be careful with "why" questions, because they can come off as challenging and put someone on the defensive. "What" questions, on the other hand, tend to convey a tone of curiosity. For example, "That's really fascinating! What was it like to . . . ?" A tip I give clients is to practice turning "why" questions into "what" questions.

No matter which tips you take away from this chapter, remember that you don't need to put on an act when it comes to flirting. You'll naturally feel more confident and forge stronger connections when you focus on how to showcase your most genuine and respectful self on dates, rather than worrying about the "right" lines to say or moves to make.

Chapter 14

"I'm Dating an Extrovert, and It's Challenging"

The social aspects of dating are not the only thing that can make it challenging for introverts. Trying to understand the person you're dating and their preference for introversion or extroversion is not easy, either. As I mentioned in part 1, very few people are completely introverted or completely extroverted. Most people fall somewhere on the spectrum, and you won't know where a romantic interest lies until you spend some time with them.

Here's the Story

Tamika and Jamal, a couple who had recently moved in together, came into their first session not even looking at each other, and the energy in the room felt very tense. I pointed out both of these things to them, and Jamal finally said, "She just blew up at me for no reason and then said I wasn't doing what she needed."

"Well, you aren't," Tamika responded angrily.

"I would if you would just tell me what I can do before exploding at me," Jamal replied just as angrily.

"I've told you a thousand times already! Just slow down!" she exclaimed, exasperated.

I finally interjected with reflection statements to try to understand both sides. "What I'm hearing is that Jamal, you experienced Tamika just blowing up at you for no reason, and Tamika, your experience is that you've already told Jamal what you need?"

"YES!" they both yelled at the same moment, looking at me with relieved expressions.

After a few moments of relaxation exercises, I was able to get Jamal and Tamika to tell me more about their relationship in a calmer way.

"I really enjoy spending time with our friends, like dinner parties or game nights. It hurts when Tamika doesn't want to join," Jamal said.

I discovered two things after further conversation with Jamal: First, the "friends" were actually Jamal's friends from before he met Tamika; and second, Tamika didn't really hang out with anyone, including her own friends. For Tamika, time spent with Jamal (and even her own friends) meant short lunch dates or a night in watching Netflix.

Let's Break It Down

This scenario is common when introverts and extroverts get together. Despite the tense start to our session, Tamika and Jamal had a great relationship. Unfortunately, their innie-outie traits were creating conflict. Jamal was a typical extrovert—acting quickly, making decisions, and just being fast in general. Tamika was becoming overwhelmed and did tell Jamal this. But there was a communication mismatch because they had such different styles, and Tamika eventually exploded due to her frustration.

Your extroverted partner is constantly making quick decisions, speeding through tasks, talking fast, reacting quickly, or just not slowing down. Eventually, you start to feel overwhelmed and drained from having to quickly process your partner's actions. The next thing you know, you and your partner are in a huge fight, with you feeling that your needs have not been respected and your partner wondering what happened.

This is not uncommon when the introvert's needs are not being met for one reason or another. Perhaps they're not stating their needs or they think they've stated them, but the extrovert has not received the message. Eventually, like a volcano under pressure, a buildup of emotions leads to an explosion.

Tamika and Jamal also had very different needs for social time and alone time, and Tamika was feeling like Jamal having his friends over was an intrusion into shared space. As we know, extroverts enjoy time with others and often schedule a lot of it, while introverts enjoy time alone or socializing with a few close people in a quiet setting. It's also common for an extrovert's social circle to become a part of the introvert's social circle. This does not change the fact that the introvert still needs time to recharge.

Jamal was inviting people into the space where Tamika found solitude and sanctuary from the outside world. From Jamal's viewpoint, Tamika was not interested in spending time with him and his friends; in reality, Tamika just had a different appetite for being social and needed more time and space to recharge.

Even in the earliest stage of dating, issues can arise between introverts and extroverts. An introvert may like someone who wants to go to parties and participate in activities that use up a lot of social energy. The introvert may go along with this for a while, and in some ways, letting the extrovert make the decisions *can* be advantageous, because the extrovert gets social time and the introvert doesn't have to overexert themselves in planning activities. However, the introvert's social fatigue will eventually show. This can lead to the extrovert questioning whether their introverted partner is truly committed to the relationship. In other words, the extrovert may take it personally when it's not personal at all.

PUT IT IN PLAY

The best way to nurture the extrovert-introvert dynamic is to make an explicit effort to understand what your partner needs and then create a balance that meets the needs of both people. Understanding will take time as your relationship grows and you get to know each other better. For new or newly flowering relationships, try these tips.

Review your list of values from chapter 3. When your dating relationship progresses past the initial stages and moves on to a deeper connection, make time to review each other's values. Discuss ways you can support each other and be clear about when you need space or for things to slow down.

Create a plan for socializing. This might include:

→ Talking with each other before inviting a large group of people over

→ Setting aside certain days of the week where neither of you receives visitors at home

→ Discussing when it's all right for the extrovert to go out with others and for the introvert to stay home alone

→ Planning for social time instead of last-minute activities

→ Making a room in your living space that's just for the introvert and that guests are not allowed to enter; that way, the introvert can retreat and have uninterrupted recharge time when others are visiting

Plan dates the other person will enjoy. This can help an extrovert-introvert couple prevent one-sided decision-making. You can adapt the date jar I described in chapter 8 to include two different colors of paper. On one color paper, the introvert writes down their ideas for great dates; on the other color, the extrovert writes down their ideas. Each week, one person takes the lead to schedule a date for the week. But here's the twist: The introvert picks a date the extrovert added to the jar, and vice versa. This will help each plan something with the other person in mind.

Schedule some time out. If you are dating an extrovert, taking some time out in the day—be it 15 minutes or a few hours—can help you recharge your battery so you aren't overextending yourself. The key here is to be upfront and communicate with your partner about your need for alone time, so they don't misread it as a lack of interest in spending time with them.

REFLECT ON IT

Although the extrovert-introvert dynamic can be fulfilling and even have some advantages for an introvert, such as access to social opportunities or having a partner who can easily make decisions, couples can also experience challenges. Reflect on a relationship you've had or are having with an extrovert. If you experienced challenges, can you think about how the suggestions here can be useful to help you both work through them? Can you see yourself doing these things with future partners? Make a plan for how you will address possible challenges with a future extrovert partner, so you have your plan ready before things get difficult.

Chapter 15

"I'm Dating Another Introvert, and It's Challenging"

Although dating another introvert may be easier than dating an extrovert, these relationships still have their own unique challenges. When I see introvert couples in my office, they often describe a lack of excitement in their relationship and are looking for ways to spice things up, or they report feeling smothered by their partner. Let's take a closer look at these challenges.

Here's the Story

Selena scored so high on the introversion spectrum that she described her dream lifestyle as living in a large house where she never had to leave or be around others. She would have a home gym, an entertainment room, a garden, and a pool, and she would get all her groceries delivered.

Although quiet, she was also quite direct. She came to me because the man she had been dating for a few months, Dominic, wanted to spend all his free time with her. "I've started to feel like Dominic has no friends or life outside of us hanging out," she confided. "He's constantly planning things for us to do weekend after weekend. He never even asks if I'm available."

While Selena had initially been excited to meet someone she clicked with, she had begun to feel smothered by Dominic. "We've known each other for a month, and I feel like his therapist at times, with all this deep emotional stuff he shares and needing me to give him advice or support. When I mention plans to work on my projects or see a friend, he acts so hurt and seems to think I don't like him."

It wasn't the first time Selena had experienced an issue dating another introvert. In her previous relationship, she'd been with someone who'd been more independent than Dominic. This had created some distance between them, to the point where they were only seeing each other once a month even though they had enough spare time to hang out more. It seemed like Selena had gone from one side of the double-edged sword to the other.

Let's Break It Down

Introvert Selena met another introvert, which is why they clicked at first. But Dominic was beginning to rely on her for all his emotional support very early on in the dating relationship. Although Selena and Dominic had their own social networks before they began dating, when they began to spend more time together, he saw his friends less and focused his attention on Selena because it was less draining for him to spend all his social energy on one person.

PUT IT IN PLAY

If you find yourself in a relationship with an introvert, remember to nurture your individuality in the relationship, including scheduling time with each other and time away from each other. Both partners should try to:

→ Stay in touch with your own social group.

→ Keep separate friend time with your own friends and make regular friend dates.

→ Enjoy hobbies without each other to allow for time apart and new and interesting conversation about your individual lives.

→ Schedule regular relationship check-ins to see if things are stagnating.

Finally, remember not to depend on your partner for all of your emotional needs. This is why maintaining your social network and friend group is important even when you are dating or in a relationship. It not only allows for time apart but also enables others in your life to support you. It's also important to learn how to support your own emotional needs, such as self-reassurance and trusting yourself to make decisions.

REFLECT ON IT

If you related to one or both of Selena's dating experiences and you see it happening in your relationship, make changes now! If you're in a relationship where things have stagnated, do you need to schedule relationship check-ins with your partner and explore ways to move past the stagnation, such as scheduling friend dates or starting that new solo hobby you've been considering? Do you or your partner rely too much on the other for emotional support? Make a list of people you could talk to about your concerns or write down ways you could tell your partner about your concerns about how much emotional support they need from you.

Chapter 16

"I Keep Missing the Red Flags"

Introverts can be like sponges, soaking up everything that's happening around them. Being such a good listener and more easily picking up on the feelings of those around you, you may be tuned in to the needs of others and sublimating your own needs. At the same time, the tendency to retreat to a rich inner world can lead to romanticizing a new love interest and missing red flags. In this chapter, we'll look at common warning signs to watch for to avoid falling into an unhealthy relationship.

Here's the Story

Yuriko, a very self-motivated woman in her 40s, scheduled an appointment with me to discuss her problems with dating. She told me about several people she had met. I asked, "How often do people come to you and just start talking about their worries?"

"Often," she responded, then said she wondered what prompted me to ask that.

I continued, "Do you ever get a chance to talk about what worries you as well?"

Yuriko shook her head. "Not really."

"I also wonder if this happens with dates. While there are plenty of advantages to being a great listener, sometimes people can interpret this as a sign that it's okay to unload all of their emotional drama."

Yuriko looked a bit shocked as she responded, "It's like you have cameras on all of my dates!"

As we talked more, Yuriko opened up about how she didn't always feel appreciated by the people she dated. "The last one I was interested in ended up ghosting me," she explained. "It's not like it was some random person, either. We had been hanging out for a while, and I thought they were nice. One week I noticed they started to be more distant, but whenever I messaged them to ask if they were okay, they just kept telling me they were really busy."

"I can imagine you must have felt pretty blindsided by being ghosted," I said.

"Totally," she agreed. "I was really hurt. I spent weeks thinking about things over and over. I couldn't figure out what I had done wrong."

I empathized. "The thing with ghosting is we don't know why it happens. Ghosting sucker-punches our self-worth and self-esteem and makes us questions ourselves when it might not be about us at all."

Let's Break It Down

People may naturally gravitate toward introverts because they can be great listeners. As Yuriko experienced, dates and partners may take advantage of this and not even realize it. Introverts can be such good listeners that people feel comfortable sharing their concerns. However, when you try to share your concerns or find emotional support, others, especially extroverts, may not listen as well or understand your needs, especially if you don't clearly state what you need from them.

Over time, this imbalance forces one partner to take on the emotional baggage of the other, while not having a place to unload their own baggage. This can lead to lopsided relationships where the introvert sublimates their thoughts, feelings, and needs, sometimes without even realizing it.

Coupled with a tendency to process information and analyze events in a slow and more thoughtful way, an introvert can fall into a spiral of self-doubt and self-recrimination. To soothe your fears and seek validation, you might seek reassurance from your date, who is by now in the habit of getting reassurance from you and not vice versa. If you don't break the pattern, it becomes a vicious cycle. And if you do, it could also result in your partner losing interest or seeing you as insecure or needy.

Caught up in these emotions, some introverts may miss the red flags that they are simply not compatible with a partner or that they are not being treated kindly or compassionately. This sets the scene for unhealthy and even toxic relationships.

PUT IT IN PLAY

The introvert's ability to think things through and assess a situation from various aspects can help you make better decisions when it comes to matters of the heart. But to avoid unhealthy relationships, you must become aware of what is and isn't healthy in a relationship. Let's take a look at a few aspects of relationships that are important to pay attention to.

→ **Autonomy vs. control or dependence:** Does your partner allow you space to make your own decisions and to speak your mind? Or does your partner attempt to control what you do and get upset when you try to have agency in decisions? Similarly, does your partner always need to be with you, need you to make all the decisions, or do things for them that they could do for themselves?

→ **Individuality vs. conformity:** Does your partner allow you to be your authentic self, even if this differs from their authentic self? Does your partner expect you to do the same things as them and think like them?

→ **Self-care vs. self-neglect:** Does your partner take care of their physical, emotional, and spiritual needs or do they sacrifice themselves for others' needs? What about you?

→ **Honesty and transparency vs. lying or omitting information:** Is your partner truthful about information, such as what they are doing or who they are with, and willing to share information with you? Or does your partner outright lie or withhold information that jeopardizes your self-worth or the integrity of the relationship?

→ **Addressing conflict vs. avoiding or ignoring conflict:** Does your partner engage in healthy conflict resolution? Or do they just put their head in the sand to ignore the conflict and avoid working toward a resolution?

If you feel like any of these may apply to your relationship or that these are red flags you tend to miss, here are some strategies for getting your dating back on the right track.

Get back in touch with your values. A good way to safeguard yourself from unhealthy relationships is to get in touch with your own desires and needs before trying to tend to those of a love interest. There are ways to explore this in chapter 3.

Listen, but make sure you are listened to. While the ability to listen is a superpower of introverts, it's important to remember that mutual understanding and attention is the cornerstone of a healthy relationship.

Don't avoid conflict. The amount of energy required for conflict can feel draining, but it's best to speak up if you feel disrespected and try to resolve the issue, rather than let it simmer. In the next chapter, we'll look at ways to engage in healthy and productive conflict.

Don't be afraid to end a relationship sooner rather than later. If you feel like someone isn't carrying their emotional weight or isn't treating you with kindness and compassion, it's best to walk away before feelings and commitments deepen.

REFLECT ON IT

This chapter explored some common red flags to look out for when dating or entering into a more committed relationship. Take a minute to reflect on your own experiences and whether there are red flags you may have missed in past relationships or in your current one.

→ Have you ever found yourself sublimating your own needs for those of a partner? If so, how might you get in touch with the values you outlined in chapter 3 and stay true to those values while dating?

→ Think of a time when you avoided bringing up something you were upset about just to keep the peace. Think of how you could have addressed it early on to resolve the issue, rather than letting it simmer.

→ Sometimes it can feel easier to listen to others than to put yourself in the spotlight by being listened to. Reflect on a time you may have felt this way while dating. How could it have benefited you to make your thoughts and feelings known?

Chapter 17

"I Don't Want to Start a Fight"

Conflict happens in all aspects of life and is bound to occur in relationships, too. Addressing the fact that something is wrong does not always mean a fight will ensue. When couples come to me with conflict issues, the most common source of their problem is that each person experiences or engages in conflict differently, which creates even more conflict. This chapter will explore how many introverts approach conflict and offer easy-to-use strategies to work through it with a partner.

Here's the Story

Harry, a psychologist in his early 40s, came to therapy with Mateo, a pharmacist in his late 30s. Both reported many of the traits of introversion. They had been dating for the last year and were now planning to move in with each other. They came to therapy to address how they handled conflict in their relationship.

"We love each other very much and get along really well," Harry started out, sounding slightly anxious, as if he needed to convince me.

"We just have a problem with fighting," Mateo continued, though not providing much detail.

"Tell me a little bit about your fights," I said, trying to encourage them to open up.

"Well, we bring up an issue with each other—" Mateo began, before Harry jumped in, saying, "—like a week or more after we had a disagreement."

"It always seems to be the worst time. We start to talk about it, but we never seem to find a resolution," Mateo added.

"Then we seem to argue about other things that happened a while ago and that weren't even the issue that day," Harry said, sounding exasperated and slumping deeper into the couch. "For instance, I might tell Mateo about something he said a week ago that bothered me. We start talking about it, and the next thing I know we are talking about something that bothered him a month ago. Then I mention something he did around that same time that irritated me. The funny thing is we've already talked about those issues in the past! It's like we just go down this rabbit hole and never even talk about the current situation. These fights are so exhausting, too! It seems like they can go on for hours. We've even left the house fighting and continued in the car while we're going somewhere."

"At the end of it all, I feel like Harry just pushes for a solution so we can get through the fight and move on," Mateo cautiously added, looking at Harry to see how he would respond.

"Well, it does sound like a lot, and I'm glad you both want to make this better," I interjected before they started a fight in my office. "Let's take a look at what might be happening."

Let's Break It Down

Conflict is always a source of stress, but it can be especially so for introverts. They may feel easily fatigued by the emotional energy conflict uses up, making them more likely to want to avoid it entirely. However, unresolved conflict can fester over time. A single incident might not be that big of a deal, but if several incidents go unresolved, this can create resentful partners or even end a relationship.

This buildup can lead to all the unresolved conflicts coming out at once, as happened with Harry and Mateo. When partners bring up several unresolved problems but don't address the real issue, it's called "kitchen sinking," which comes from the saying, "Everything but the kitchen sink." Harry and Mateo were doing this when they tried to talk about the current disagreement and ended up mired in past disagreements. This is unproductive, and it's overwhelming enough to engage in one conflict, never mind several at one time. Kitchen sinking also redirects attention from the concern at hand, which leaves the partners with yet another unresolved issue.

Another common pattern that I see with unproductive conflict is one person needing resolution sooner than the other, as Mateo said about Harry. This rush to resolution could be your partner responding to uncomfortable feelings such as anxiety and trying to soothe those feelings with a solution. It could also be you or your partner just wanting to avoid the conflict and the toll it takes on their energy reserves. Either way, rushing another person to resolve a conflict is counterproductive to healthy conflict resolution. One partner might have to slow down to let the other catch up, which can be very uncomfortable.

PUT IT IN PLAY

If you find yourself avoiding conflict to keep the peace or find it difficult to resolve a conflict, these strategies will help.

Remember, conflict can be healthy and productive. Don't always view it as negative. In fact, conflict can make partners stop and actively listen to each other's point of view. You and your partner might not always see eye to eye on everything; use these times to learn more about your partner and their perspective.

Listen with empathy. As you know, listening is a strength of many introverts. This is a major asset when it comes to talking through and resolving conflict. Make space for your partner to get their point across and try rephrasing what they've said to show them you've listened and understood their feelings. Remember, it's possible to validate someone's feelings without necessarily agreeing with them.

Try the time-out technique. This is of my most favorite exercises to use with clients who are having trouble engaging in healthy and productive conflict. If you find yourself in the heat of an argument, it allows each partner to cool off, process their thoughts, and reach a resolution.

1. Call the time-out. This can be done with an agreed-upon nonverbal gesture, such as putting your hands on your head.

2. Go to separate time-out spaces for 30 minutes, such as different rooms in a home. During this time, engage in self-care (such as journaling, letter writing, or listening to music) or self-soothing exercises (such as meditation or light movement such as stretching or yoga). Avoid merely distracting yourself with electronics.

3. During your time-out, think about what you want to say to your partner or what you were trying to say. You could also think about what you were hearing them say that may have activated your anxiety. Saying it out loud or writing a letter is good for this.

4. After 30 minutes, reconvene and begin talking out the conflict, using active and empathetic listening and I statements. I statements are things like, "What I heard you saying is _____" or, "What I am trying to say is _____" or, "When I found out about _____, I felt _____."

5. If you can't reach a resolution, try extending the time-out for another 30 minutes or table the conversation until the next day.

REFLECT ON IT

There are ways to have healthy and productive conflict. As an introvert, your ability to listen is a definite strength, and taking a time-out can help you process your thoughts. Consider how the following reflections can help you resolve rather than avoid conflicts when they arise.

→ What is your default conflict style? How is this different from your current or previous partner's style? Remember, it's important to respect that your partner's personality may differ from yours.

→ What might a conflict resolution plan look like that works for you and your partner? How can you use this consistently when you have a conflict?

→ If you are experiencing frequent disagreements, it might be helpful to have a regular check-in weekly or monthly to explore issues. This can prevent unresolved conflict from building up over time and turning into kitchen sinking.

Chapter 18

"I Love My Solitude, but I Don't Want to Be Alone"

Enjoying solitude and being in a relationship are not mutually exclusive. In this chapter, we'll look at how other introverts have successfully balanced solitude while dating.

Here's the Story

Aliyah, a quirky and bubbly woman in her late 30s, had been dating Caleb, also in his late 30s, for about a year now. In contrast to Aliyah, Caleb had a reserved demeanor but was the kind of person who was easy to talk to.

Aliyah embodied traits of both extroversion and introversion. She could be the life of the party and engage in conversations with strangers without much anxiety, but she also enjoyed her solitude. Often, she talked about how much she enjoyed staying home and working on her craft projects all weekend. She was very self-sufficient, getting daily life tasks completed without much help and not fretting about doing chores for herself alone.

She told me she spent time with friends, such as girls' trips to the mountains and spa days. Caleb reported that he enjoyed spending time with Aliyah, though he also had several of his own projects that he often worked on in his downtime.

During one session, Aliyah talked about her fear of what would happen if she never found a life partner. "I'm just so afraid of being alone," she said.

Caleb listened attentively and showed genuine concern for her anxiety. I pressed her to elaborate.

"I really enjoy spending time with Caleb, though he always has projects going on. I'm just there alone, even though I know my friends would hang out with me if I asked."

"That does sound frustrating," I said with empathy. "When you paint this picture in your head, what does being alone in the future look like?"

Aliyah sat in silence reflecting on my question for what felt like an eternity. "Well, it just looks like me being alone," she eventually responded, now on the verge of tears. "It feels so lonely!"

Caleb responded, "I really like you, and I like spending time with you. I know this bothers you more than it does me. I feel really bad about it." He sounded conflicted. Caleb went on to share his own fear about how his desire for alone time was affecting his relationship so early on. "What happens if my need to be alone causes Aliyah to break up with me?" he asked, now looking fearful.

To soothe their fears and provide a light at the end of this scary tunnel, I said, "A lot of people like to have alone time. We just need to figure out what that looks like for you both."

Let's Break It Down

Often, people who express a fear of being alone are really fearing something else that is much scarier to think of, such as a fear of not having support from a partner or a fear of having to give up something important.

Humans are social creatures and often depend on one another for survival. In fact, humans cannot thrive when they are isolated and don't have human connections. Some studies, including the Bucharest Project, show that children need more than basic food and shelter to emotionally, intellectually, and physically thrive. These studies have shown that infants and toddlers do better when caregivers regularly touch and speak to them. Put simply, we humans are hardwired for connection, and this need continues throughout our lives.

A 2020 study in the *Journal of the American Academy of Psychiatry and the Law* reported on the effects of solitary confinement on prison inmates. About one-third of inmates experienced mental distress due to social isolation. While perhaps an extreme example, it illustrates how crucial social interaction is to us as humans.

In other words, while introverts need solitude for their overall well-being, they need human connection as well. The important thing is to make sure you are nurturing *both* needs. That's why going on dates even if you're unsure about a person is still beneficial (provided your boundaries for your safety and comfort are still maintained); it feeds your need for human contact until you meet "the one." Knowing yourself and your needs is also important to ensure that you are communicating your needs to your date or partner.

PUT IT IN PLAY

It's important that you honor *all* your needs, including balancing a relationship with your need for solo time. Aliyah and Caleb seem almost like two sides of the same coin; certainly, the way they balanced these two needs was very different. There are several things you can do to ensure you get your solitude and your social contact in the ways and amounts you need them.

First, when you meet someone you really like and the relationship progresses, be sure to let them know how much time you need to yourself, what this time alone looks like for you, and what you might (or might not) need from them during this time.

Second, to ensure that you get your solitude and that your partner gets the time they need with you, and to prevent too much distance in the relationship, schedule alone time and date/partner time every week. Here are a few ways to schedule this time.

→ **Carve out regular and consistent solo time:** This might be for your hobby or simply time alone at home. Consistency is key for this to become a part of your regular routine.

→ **A shared calendar:** Create one of these with your partner so you see what times are available for each other and what are the scheduled solitude times.

→ **A weekly relationship check-in:** Use this to discuss solitude time and to schedule dates for the week.

For those who have similar fears to Aliyah, here are some ways to challenge your fear-based thoughts.

→ **Become aware of your thoughts; thoughts influence your emotions.** If you are feeling fearful or scared, be aware of what thought is going through your mind at that time and how it is influencing you.

→ **Determine whether the thought is based in reality or a distortion.** Ask yourself, "How likely or unlikely is it that this could actually happen?"

▸ If the thought is unlikely and based in distortion, create a positive reframe (see chapter 5) for something that is more likely to happen.

▸ When you're reframing a distorted thought, create a plan for how to get to that positive outcome. For instance, if your goal is to have a partner later in life, create a dating plan now to work toward that goal.

REFLECT ON IT

Your social circle may be smaller, but the need to be socially connected to others is just as important as the need for alone time. When these come into conflict, you may think that you must choose one over the other. This can invoke a fear of being alone or of losing a sense of self.

Aliyah and Caleb's story will help you to differentiate between alone time and a fear of being alone. Reflecting on your personal experience:

→ Have you ever been fearful of being alone and sacrificed your need for alone time?

→ What does your alone time look like? How is it different from a fear of being alone?

→ Remember, the key to managing your introversion while dating or in a relationship is to strike a comfortable balance. It doesn't need to be an all-or-nothing equation; you can carve out quiet moments to enjoy some solitude during the week without having to forgo quality time together with your partner.

→ How do you imagine balancing time with people and solitude time? Looking at the coming week, how can you schedule both into your week?

Chapter 19

"I'm Afraid to Open Up"

The introvert's inner world can be a vulnera-ble place, which can naturally feel exposed during the dating process. Some introverts may feel this way about their outer world as well. Of course, it's okay to take your time to open up when dating. You may reach a relationship milestone, such as saying "I love you" for the first time, a little later than an extrovert might, and that's okay! However, if you find yourself having trouble opening up at all, this chapter will help you be openhearted and vulnerable in a way that feels comfortable for you.

Here's the Story

Imani had been on a few dates with Sara, whom she had met on a dating app. They met up for lunch on their first date, and on the second went to a movie and had dinner afterward. There was a lot that Imani liked about Sara: She was attractive, had a quick wit, and seemed caring and kind.

161

On their third date, Imani—a self-identified introvert—noticed that Sara was confiding in her more, showing not just her bright and happy side, but offering a glimpse into a more vulnerable part of herself, too. While Imani was touched that Sara felt comfortable enough around her to share this side, rather than putting her at ease, she found that it made her tense and more reluctant to share similar information about herself.

As their dinner date progressed, Sara told Imani about why her last job had been a colossal failure, which had led to a long period of soul-searching. "My old manager used to really get under my skin," she said after thinking about it for a beat. "She was always micromanaging everyone on our team. So much so that we used to call her the Demander in Chief!"

While this drew a laugh from Sara, Imani put her guard up a little. In truth, her previous manager had made her feel like she was an imposter in her job, which had led to her own period of soul-searching. It had been a source of shame for her, and for some reason, she couldn't open up to Sara about it. Finally, just to end the silence, she said, "I've been there with bad managers."

"How did that make you feel?" Sara asked, searching for a deeper conversation.

"Well, I think everyone on the team wanted to quit at various times," Imani replied, deflecting away from herself. "Though we stuck it out, and luckily our new manager is a dream to work with."

The waiter arrived with their dinner and the conversation moved on to lighter terrain, putting Imani at ease again, yet leaving her feeling confused by her inability to open up to Sara.

Let's Break It Down

Most people are like an onion with many layers to pull back. The outer layers are less vulnerable than the inner ones. Another analogy is your own body. You have many layers to your body that help protect the innermost vital organs. If you get a minor scratch on your skin, this doesn't cause any damage to the deeper levels, whereas a stab or a puncture wound would cause more damage deeper inside.

Everyone is like this, but introverts, being extra cautious, tend to be more so. By sharing these vulnerable parts of your life very slowly, you may feel more in control and better protected if things don't work out. However, opening up too slowly can also prevent you from progressing with dating or building relationships if others begin to feel they are not welcomed or trusted in all parts of your life.

People are inherently wired to need connection with others. Vulnerability, or the ability to show more of yourself, allows you to make deeper connections with others, which is what introverts typically seek. The risk with vulnerability is that you may be sharing tender parts of yourself that could be rejected.

Shame and fear are leading motivators to hide and protect our most vulnerable places. In her 2010 TEDxHouston talk, researcher Brené Brown said shame is about hiding oneself, and she explained how shame unravels connections. You may think, "If I open myself up and share my inner thoughts with you and you reject me for this, then I have caused myself to be alone." If reading that stung a little for you, take a moment to let it sink in before reading on.

PUT IT IN PLAY

Fear and anxiety can hold people back, as we try to protect ourselves from getting hurt or losing a connection with others. However, it can also prevent you from finding a deeper connection with a partner, as we saw with Imani. Let's look at ways you can balance opening and being vulnerable in a way that makes you more comfortable with new people.

Accept your imperfections. No one is perfect. In fact, many of your imperfections are what make you unique and intriguing. One way to work toward opening up is to accept that you and your life (and your future partner!) will never be perfect.

Realize you're not alone. When you get caught up in your problems, you forget that other people have their own issues, too. If you've ever found yourself scrolling past picture-perfect couples on Instagram, you've likely had feelings like, "Their life is perfect, but look at mine." Remember, what you see on the outside doesn't always reflect the reality. Sharing your insecurities and fears with family and friends can be a great way to feel less burdened by them, and you'll more than likely find they've been through something similar.

Practice empathy. Empathy is the ability to recognize what another person is feeling or experiencing because you have gone through the same or a similar situation or experienced the same or similar feelings. For instance, when you tell someone, "Hey, no big deal! I totally get it," you are practicing empathy. The caveat is that we humans are often better at showing empathy for others than we are ourselves. While you practice empathy for others, don't forget to include yourself.

Cheer yourself on. Being your own cheerleader means offering yourself unconditional love and encouragement. For instance, before a date, you might give yourself a pep talk, including words of encouragement and reminder tips about how to manage your anxiety or make small talk.

Create a self-care plan. When things don't go as you hope, be sure to have a self-care plan to soothe your wounded heart. This could include calling a close friend, taking a walk in your favorite park, a bubble bath, a meditation session, or anything that takes care of you.

REFLECT ON IT

For some, this chapter might have been hard to read. To be honest, it was a little hard to write. Because I'm not perfect, it was a nice reminder of how *I* still have work to do. While writing, I took my own advice and practiced self-care, such as taking breaks when things got too deep and cheering myself on as a reminder that I can still handle stress. Take some time now to check in with yourself and see how you can show yourself some love and empathy. For example:

→ Sit in a quiet room and take slow, deep breaths. Notice where you feel tension in your body.

→ Go for a 10-minute walk and take a moment to *really* notice five things you see, three things you hear, and two things you smell.

→ Write yourself a love note expressing gratitude to yourself or listing three to five things that make you proud about yourself.

→ Look at your weekend schedule and plan at least one activity that is all for you and no one else.

It's worth checking back in on these self-care practices as you continue your dating journey. When you are kind and caring to yourself, you set a solid foundation to weather the ups and downs you may experience and to believe you are worthy of love and acceptance, not for who think you are supposed to be, but for who you really are.

Resources

Resources About Introversion

Books

The Introvert Advantage: How Quiet People Can Thrive in an Extrovert World, by Marti Olsen Laney, PsyD, Workman Publishing, 2002

The Mindful Self-Compassion Workbook: A Proven Way to Accept Yourself, Build Inner Strength, and Thrive, by Kristin Neff, PhD, and Christopher Germer, PhD, The Guilford Press, 2018

The Secret Lives of Introverts: Inside Our Hidden World, by Jenn Granneman, Skyhorse Publishing, 2017

The Seven Habits of Highly Effective People: Powerful Lessons in Personal Change, by Stephen R. Covey, Free Press, 2004

Online Resources

Franklin Covey Mission Statement and Values Builder is a tool to help you find what you believe in. You can learn more at MSB.FranklinCovey .com.

Introvert, Dear is community dedicated to introverts, with articles on everything from the science of introversion to love, dating, and parenthood as an introvert. You can read more at IntrovertDear.com.

Introversion Personality Assessments

Eysenck Personality Inventory

GoGovernment.org/test/eysencks-personality-inventory-epi -extroversionintroversion

The Eysenck Personality Inventory measures two pervasive, independent dimensions of personality: extroversion-introversion and neuroticism-stability. This is a self-administered test.

STAR Introversion test

Blogs.ScientificAmerican.com/beautiful-minds/what-kind-of -introvert-are-you

This is a self-administered test to find out where you stand on the scale of Social, Thinking, Anxious, and Restrained introversion.

Myers-Briggs Type Indicator assessment

MBTIOnline.com

This is the official MBTI instrument, offered online by The Myers-Briggs Company. It costs $49.95.

Conversation Cards

Conversation Cards

This deck from CC Playing Cards is great for dates, friends, and family. There are 200 thought-provoking conversation starters presented on a deck of classic playing cards. They're available from many online retailers.

Heart2Heart by TiffinTalk

TiffinTalk.com/cards-and-services/h2h

This fun and sexy card deck is for couples only.

Our Moments: Couples Edition

Our-Moments.co/products/couples-edition

This deck is designed to help couples get to know each other.

Where Should We Begin: A Game of Stories
EstherPerel.com/where-should-we-begin-the-game
This deck from psychotherapist Esther Perel is designed to introduce playfulness and storytelling into a date or get-together.

Dating, Relationships, and Mental Health Resources

American Association of Marriage and Family Therapists
AAMFT.org
A professional association for the field of marriage and family therapy. You can find a therapist in your area.

American Association of Sexuality Educators, Counselors, and Therapists
AASECT.org
A national organization providing up-to-date and evidence-based information about relationships and sexuality. You can find a therapist in your area.

Just a Little Nudge
ALittleNudge.com
An online dating and coaching service to help you navigate the stressors of online dating.

Psychology Today
PsychologyToday.com
An online source of mental health information, including a searchable database of therapists.

References

American Psychiatric Association. (2018). "What are Personality Disorders?" Psychiatry.org/patients-families/personality-disorders/what-are-personality-disorders

Booker, Karene. (2013). "Extroverts have more sensitive brain-reward system." *Cornell Chronicle*. news.Cornell.edu/stories/2013/07/brain-chemistry-plays-role-extroverts

Brown, Brené. (2010). "The Power of Vulnerability." TEDxHouston. TED.com/talks/brene_brown_the_power_of_vulnerability?language=en#t-263462

Cain, Susan. (2013). *Quiet: The Power of Introverts in a World That Can't Stop Talking*. New York: Crown Publishing Group.

Covey, Stephen R. (2020). *The 7 Habits of Highly Effective People*. New York: Simon & Schuster.

Cristol, Hope. (2021). "What Is Dopamine?" WebMD. WebMD.com/mental-health/what-is-dopamine

Dahl, Melissa. (2020). "Apparently There are Four Kinds of Introversion." *The Cut*. TheCut.com/article/apparently-there-are-four-kinds-of-introversion.html

Davis, Jarrod. (2019). "The Introvert Hangover Is Real." *Mind Café*. Medium.com/mind-cafe/the-introvert-hangover-is-real-d68f3325a67

GoGovernment. (2020). "Eysenck's Personality Inventory." GoGovernment.org/test/eysencks-personality-inventory-epi-extroversionintroversion

Granneman, Jenn. (2017). *The Secret Lives of Introverts: Inside Our Hidden World.* New York: Skyhorse Publishing.

Hall, Jeffrey A. (2013). *The Five Flirting Styles: Use the Science of Flirting to Attract the Love You Really Want.* New York: Harlequin.

Houston, Elaine. (2021). "Introvert vs. Extrovert: A Look at the Spectrum and Psychology." *Positive Psychology.* PositivePsychology.com /introversion-extroversion-spectrum

Jung, Carl G. (2014). *The Collected Works of C. G. Jung.* Edited and Translated by Gerhard Adler and R.F.C. Hull. Princeton, NJ: Princeton University Press.

Kaufman, Scott B. (2014). "What Kind of Introvert Are You?" *Scientific American.* blogs.ScientificAmerican.com/beautiful-minds/what-kind-of-introvert-are-you

Laney, Marti Olsen. (2002). *The Introvert Advantage: How Quiet People Can Thrive in an Extrovert World.* New York: Workman Publishing.

Leonard, Jayne. (2020). "What are the effects of solitary confinement on health?" *Medical News Today.* MedicalNewsToday.com/articles /solitary-confinement-effects#mental-health-effects

McHugh, Adam S. (2015). *The Listening Life: Embracing Attentiveness in a World of Distraction.* Westmont, IL: InterVarsity Press.

McLeod, Saul. (2017). "Theories of Personality." *Simply Psychology.* SimplyPsychology.org/personality-theories.html

Oxford English Dictionary. (2021). Oxford University Press. OED.com

Rosenfeld, Michael J., Reuben J. Thomas, and Sonia Hausen. (2019). "Disintermediating your friends: How online dating in the United States displaces other ways of meeting." *Proceedings of the National Academy of Sciences.* PNAS.org/content/116/36/17753 /tab-figures-data

Turner, Summer. (2019). "Stop Telling Introverts to Leave Their Comfort Zone! What to Say Instead . . ." Summer Turner. SuccessForIntrovertedWomen.com/stop-telling-introverts -to-leave-their-comfort-zone-what-to-say-instead

Waltman, S., and E. Murphy. (2016). "Play the Script till the End." Psychology Tools. PsychologyTools.com/play-the-script-till -the-end

Weir, Kirsten. (2014). "The Lasting Impact of Neglect." American Psychological Association. APA.org/monitor/2014/06/neglect

Index

Present moment awareness, 98–99
Profiles, creating dating, 109–110

R

Red flags, 143–147
Rejection, fear of, 35
Relationships
   dating throughout, 101–102
   healthy vs. unhealthy, 143–147

S

Secret Lives of Introverts, The
      (Granneman), 61
Selectiveness, 26–27, 57–63
Self-care, 164–165
Seven Habits of Highly Effective
      People, The (Covey), 67
Shyness, 13–15

Silence, 95–99
Small talk, 27–28, 75–78, 121–125
Social anxiety, 13–15
Solitude, 99–102, 155–159
STAR acronym, 7
Stereotypes, 11–12

T

Time-out technique for conflict
      resolution, 152–153
Turner, Summer, 35

V

Values, 40–42, 47–51

W

Waltman, Scott, 37

Acknowledgments

Thank you to all my friends and colleagues who supported me along this journey. When I doubted myself, you were there with encouragement, guidance, and feedback. I want to thank Jenn and Gordon for being sounding boards the countless times I got writer's block! Thanks also to my editor, Adrian, for supporting a newbie writer.

Finally, this process wouldn't have been possible without the clients who entrusted me with their dating and relationship needs. It is a privilege that you share your stories with me. Thank you for trusting that I could provide support and guidance during your unique journeys.

About the Author

 Courtney Geter, LMFT-S, CST, is a licensed marriage and family therapist and certified sex therapist. She received her degree in child and family development from the University of Georgia and a master's degree in marriage and family therapy from Drexel University. She is also a certified sex therapist with the American Association of Sexuality Educators, Counselors, and Therapists.

Courtney founded Atlanta Therapeutic Collective, a group practice providing sex and relationship therapy. She also founded Papaya Parties, which holds adult sex ed events and workshops.

Courtney is a clinical fellow with the American Association for Marriage and Family Therapy and a lifetime member of the LGBTQ Therapist Resource. She is also the creator and producer of the *Let's Talk Sex* podcast, providing fun and informative information on sexuality. It can be found on her website and SoundCloud.

You can find Courtney at SexAndRelationshipTherapist.com and on Instagram @SexTherapistAtl. Her group practice is at AtlantaTherapeuticCollective.com.